Change *Almost* Anything in 21 Days

Expanded Edition
Recharge Your Life with the Power of Over 500 Affirmations

Ruth Fishel

Illustrated by Bonny Van de Kamp

Health Communications, Inc.
Deerfield Beach, Florida
www.bcibooks.com

Library of Congress Cataloging-in-Publication Data

Fishel, Ruth
 Change almost anything in 21 days : recharge your life with the
power of over 500 affirmations / Ruth Fishel ; illustrated by Bonny Van
de Kamp.—Expanded ed.
  p. cm.
 ISBN 0-7573-0067-7
 1. Affirmations. 2. Change (Psychology) I. Title.

BF697.5.S47 F57 2002
158.1—dc21

               2002032920

©2003 Ruth Fishel
ISBN 0-7573-0067-7

Publisher: Health Communications, Inc.
     3201 S.W. 15th Street
     Deerfield Beach, FL 33442-8190

R-03-03

Cover design by Lisa Camp
Inside book design by Dawn Von Strolley Grove

Contents

5

6

7

With Gratitude

I am so very grateful to all the people who have made this book possible.

A huge thank you to Sandy Bierig, who has been an editor, supporter and contributor to all my books. Thanks for all your patience and love.

It has been a joy to work with the very gifted Bonny Van de Kamp again. Bonny has been an important part of many of my books, dating back to 1987 with my first book, *The Journey Within*.

To all the wonderful people who have contributed their special affirmations and for sharing their powerful experiences: Dorna Allen, Sharon Anderson, Mary Jane Beach, Karen Beaton, Lisa Boone, Nan Cardos, Caryn Case, Thaisa Clapham, Maureen Corrigan, Dale Cotter, Leslie Fabian, Joseph Foote, Sue Howe, Mersh Lubel Kanis, Margie Levine, Darlene Neimeyer, Mindy Ruch, Diane Webster and Nancy Wellington.

A huge thanks for all who helped with the first edition to make the second edition possible: Debbie Boisseau, Brian Bierig, Jane Brown, Nicki Garner and Barbara Thomas.

I'm extremely grateful to Peter Vegso at Health Communications for seeing the value in the first pocket edition of *Change Almost Anything in 21 Days* and encouraging me to expand it.

I am deeply grateful to have had so many wonderful teachers over the years, including every client, retreat and workshop attendee. I cannot name them all, but you will always be in my heart and have my gratitude.

And a special thank you to Bill W. and Dr. Bob, without whom I would not be alive.

Prologue

A small group of tired, discouraged-looking people gathered together, waiting to be told where to go. They had just arrived and were confused and disoriented. Suddenly they saw a bright light and heard a gentle voice.

"Welcome."

Everyone looked up.

"You have come a long way," the voice continued. "And you have had many exhausting, painful experiences. Easy does it. Know that you are safe. You have nothing to fear. You are beautiful human beings and I love you."

The crowd stirred and looked around, trying to find the source of the beautiful voice.

"This is the time to search deeply into your hearts and find your regrets," the voice went on.

"Some are easy to see. Others are buried deep inside, hidden from your consciousness. Find them all. Be honest with yourselves. Don't be afraid. Now is your chance to clear out all those blocks that stood in the way of pure joy and love. Regrets serve no other purpose than to keep you stuck in the past.

"What are your regrets? There's nothing to fear."

A brave soul said, "It's so painful to think of regrets. Do I really have to?"

"If you want to be free to move on," the voice answered gently. "You are ready to move on or you wouldn't be here listening to me. As the saying goes, 'Pain is inevitable. Suffering is optional.' I think you're ready to give up your suffering."

At that, each person looked up, surprised. Some of the tiredness left their faces. They were standing a bit straighter. They listened, waiting for more.

There was silence.

"I wish I had a better sex life," a graying sixty-or-so man said sheepishly.

"Good," responded the voice.

"I wish I had taken better care of myself," whispered a heavy, middle-aged woman with a beautiful face.

"Wonderful!"

"I wish I had more money."

"I wish I had gone to college."

"I wish I had been less fearful."

"I wish I had been a better person."

"I wish I hadn't drank so much alcohol."

Once they began, regrets poured out until there was finally silence.

"Look a bit deeper," said the voice.

Silence . . . and then,

"I wish I had been more compassionate."

"I wish I had been a better parent."

"I wish I hadn't taken drugs."

Silence.

One man stood alone, not participating. The crowd slowly turned to him. The faces in the crowd were soft and looked younger, and they were all smiling.

"Come on."

"No."

"It feels good just to say it."

"No."

"You can do this," they encouraged.

"I . . . I never took a chance. I took a job out of high school, never went to college, never changed my job and never grew. I was always afraid to try something new, and now it's too late." He burst into tears and the crowd gathered around him and held him.

"It's never too late," said the gentle voice. "There is always time. I have given you all the ability to change and the gift of free will. You can go back and make different changes if you wish. You have all been born with a very special gift that you haven't fully used. When you wake up, you will find simple instructions on how to turn around your regrets. Go now. Go with my love. And above all, love yourselves and each other."

Welcome to the Wonderful, Life-Changing World of Affirmations

We live in a world where change is inevitable. Many of the changes are predictable. Spring turns to summer, turns to fall, turns to winter and then to spring again. Over and over again. Babies are born and grandparents die. Students pass one grade and move on to the next one.

And then there are unpredictable changes. A suicide bomber enters a nightclub and in one split second forty people are dead. Someone wins the lottery and is suddenly a millionaire. A drunk driver crosses the median strip and wipes out a family of six. A relative dies and leaves you a house on the water. An airplane crashes into the Twin Towers, and the world is never the same. The IRS finds a mistake in your tax return and sends you a check for $1,500. You go to the doctor with the flu and find out you have a life-threatening disease.

In one split second we can find ourselves in a situation that results in an irrevocable change, and we feel powerless. We might even come to the conclusion that life runs us, rather than us being in charge of our lives.

While there are incidents and situations that the universe decides for us, we can usually change how we feel inside. Aside from the unpredictable and predictable life changes, we can be in charge of a great deal of what happens in our life, more than most people imagine.

We do have the power to change.

But what about sickness, you might ask. Can I write and say and think affirmations and I will recover? Maybe yes and maybe no. We can't guarantee it, although some people swear that affirmations have worked that way for them. Doctors Larry Dossey, Bernie Siegel and Jeanne Achterberg are only a few who have proven that affirmations, visualizations, prayer and positive thinking have been responsible for curing life-threatening diseases.

What I can offer is that whatever you are going through, affirmations can help you have a better attitude and help you to feel better mentally, physically and spiritually. Wayne Dyer tells us that affirmations can help us change our focus from what we don't have and what's missing to love, gratitude and forgiveness, thus paving the way for positive changes.

Introduction

*It takes only one person to
change your life . . . you.*

Ruth Casey

Dear Reader,

Are there parts of your life you would like to change? Are there places you would like to go? Things you would like to do? Have you been looking for a purpose in your life? Do you sometimes wonder why some people seem to get all the breaks when you get very few or none at all? Does life ever seem like an ongoing struggle? How many times have you wanted something to happen in your life and it didn't? Or even if almost everything is going just the way you want, is there something you would like to add or subtract from your life?

If you can say yes to any of these questions, there's a very good chance that this book can help you. I say, *can* help you, not *will* help you, because whether it does or doesn't is up to you! The techniques in this book definitely can help you. But you have to be willing to change. Or, at least be willing to be willing to change. Do you really want to let go of the old ways that haven't worked to find the courage to try new ones?

We can't always get what we want. Life just doesn't work that way. And, what we want is not always the best for us. But by making only one difference in your life, your life can get better. You can have more of what you want. You can let go of some of your struggle. The question is, are you willing to put your energy and commitment into making a change?

As soon as you become willing to try the simple techniques in this book, incredible transformations will begin to happen in your life. You will quickly see the power and the possibilities that lie ahead of you.

A smaller pocket version of this book was published in 2001. Because so many people e-mailed, wrote and talked to me to let me know how much the book helped them, this expanded version shouted to be written. If you read the first version, you will discover many more ideas and techniques here to help you change. The affirmation index has been expanded by over 150 affirmations. And if you're new to this process, you are in for a wonderful surprise.

I've seen people find new jobs, homes, cars, careers, hidden talents, attitudes, friendships and relationships. I've witnessed others experience remarkable results, including healing from major illnesses and no longer needing medication for diabetes and attention deficit disorder. Addicts have become clean and sober, stopped smoking, given up gambling and over-spending. Students have passed exams they were sure they would fail. Fights have been avoided. Resentments have been healed. Many, many people have found peace of mind, improved their self-esteem, made a deeper spiritual connection and established a more meaningful purpose for their lives.

So go for it! Have some fun with this book and make changes that will add quality, serenity, happiness and joy to your life. You're worth it!

With Love and Peace,
Ruth

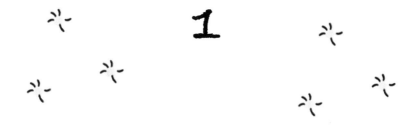

1

Change Almost
Anything in
21 Days

Many years ago, while I was struggling to end my active addiction to alcohol, a very wise man told me that we can change almost anything we want to change in our lives. He said we can change our name, our location, our careers, our relationships, just about everything, for one day. He said that most things could be changed back if we didn't like the change. I thought, *That's easy for him to say,* but my struggle continued. *How,* I wondered, *would change happen for me?*

When I was a child, my father instilled deeply in me the message that "Ruth can do anything." Over and over he repeated the story about how I had taught myself to ski. He told and retold it to anyone who would listen about how every time I fell down, I would pick myself up and start over. He said that was how I could do anything I wanted to do: Stay with the task I wanted to accomplish, and if I fell, simply pick myself up and start over again. Because of hearing this message over and over for so many years, I thought I really could do just about anything. But, that was until the compulsion to drink became stronger than I could handle and I couldn't stop, no matter how I tried.

Finally, with the help of many other recovering alcoholics, I was introduced to the concept of a Power greater than myself. The idea was extraordinarily difficult for me to grasp at first, because I was such an extremely independent and arrogant person and believed that God was simply a crutch used by very weak people. *Believe in God if you want to*, I thought, *but not me! That's not what I need!* However, nothing else was working. I simply could not stop drinking. Finally, after much pain and despair, I turned to this Power and humbly asked for help. The miracle happened. I soon lost my desire to drink.

I came to believe in a Power in the universe that I could not see or touch. I knew for certain It was there. I saw It at work in the miracle of the changing seasons, the birth of my children, a seed becoming a flower. I saw the results in the changes in other people's lives. Today I call that Power God.

Hungry to learn more, I went on to study about the power of prayer and meditation, intentions and the power of words. I learned about the wonderful concept of the power of affirmations and the power of 21 days. Marvelous things began to happen. I became more confident. I overcame my fear of public speaking. I was able to help in the opening of an alcoholism treatment program for women when all odds were against us. My life began to change as I developed my ability to use these powerful techniques. I also learned that it is not possible to change everything. There are some things, like winning the Olympics at the age of sixty-two or becoming an opera singer if you are tone deaf, that are out of the realm of our ability to alter, no matter what we do, and, with time and experience, we learn to accept our limitations. However, as we grow in our practice and become more open to allowing these powers to work in our lives, we discover that even if we wish for one result, it might not be in our best interests to have it, because something better might be waiting for us. We learn to trust the process of growth and change.

Eventually, I taught and wrote about these subjects, because they work! My intention in writing this particular book is to take everything I know about affirmations, everything that I have learned from teachers, clients, workshop and retreat participants, friends and my own experience, and put it all in one place. This book is meant to be a vehicle for transformation. Anyone can pick it up and find the subject they wish to change and learn how to make it happen. After many years of teaching affirmations and utilizing them in my own life, I have found that one of the greatest barriers to successful outcomes is that people have difficulty correctly wording affirmations to achieve the results they want.

What is unique in *Change Almost Anything in 21 Days* is that there are more than 500 affirmations alphabetized according to topic. You can find a positive, powerful affirmation for almost any subject you want or need to change. For example, if you're nervous about a job interview or an upcoming exam, simply look up *fear* or *confidence* in the index. Do you want to lose weight? Check out *food* or *addiction*. If the affirmation you find doesn't feel quite perfect, rewrite it in your own words, remembering to use the five rules for successful affirmations discussed later in this book.

Experiment with affirmations. Experience their magnetism as they connect you with the power and energy of the universe. Know there is a power for good and love in the universe and watch how it can bring miraculous changes into your life!

Intentions

*Intentions set into process
every aspect of your life.*

Gary Zukav

Change begins with the intention to change. In the *Seat of the Soul,* Gary Zukav gives us the following example of intending to change your job. "As the intention to leave your present job emerges into your consciousness, you begin to open yourself up to the possibility of working somewhere else or doing something else. You begin to feel less and less at home with what you are doing. Your higher self has begun the search for your next job."

I remember a time when I was looking for a new convertible. While I was in college, I had a very old convertible. As my finances improved over the years, I was able to purchase newer cars and finally could afford a new car. This was around the time that the Mustang and the Firebird convertibles first came out. I had not been aware of them until someone told me they were great cars. As I drove around town I began seeing them everywhere. My children were very young and when we went on errands they would yell out, "There's a Firebird!" and "There's a Mustang!" I had created an intention, and my awareness grew. It was as if the universe was providing me with plenty of opportunities to make a decision.

Volition is the mental urge
or signal which precedes an action.

Joseph Goldstein

So we begin with an intention. Something we want to add, reduce, change or let go. We *intend* to make it happen.

June is a true miracle, a poster woman for affirmations. When she was diagnosed with metastasized breast cancer, it sent her and her family reeling. Fortunately, June had a strong intention to live.

She wrote, "That I'm still here physically almost a year later is a testament to modern medical science. That I'm facing each day with hope, acceptance, inner independence and an eagerness to learn from this amazing experience is in part due to my renewed association with your affirmation meditation group. I needed something very basic when I joined the group five months after diagnosis.

"Though tolerating chemotherapy extremely well, the reality of my situation could be daunting at times. I needed something to help shift my focus from treating the disease that afflicts my body to treating the whole me. I needed to

remember that I am not alone on this journey. This was
my intention, and affirmations clarify intentions. We came
up with what turned out to be a very powerful affirmation
for me, which helped me accept my life as it is today with
growing peace and a great deal of joy:

*"'Healing' energy is flowing through every
cell in my body with every breath I take."*

When June completed writing her affirmation for 21 days,
she found another powerful affirmation that was
extremely helpful for her:

*"I am letting go of doubt, fear, anger and
distrust and quietly accept the unknown."*

Why not take some time now to think about what you
would like to change in your life. You can write your
thoughts down, and then, with the succeeding steps in
this book, you will learn how you can make the change.

*Is there something you would like to add, such as more
meaning in your job, a new relationship or a deeper
spiritual connection?*

_____

_____

_____

_____

_____

Is there something you would like to reduce, such as weight, negative thinking or fear?

_____

_____

_____

_____

_____

Is there something you would like to change, such as where you live, your job or your attitude?

_____

_____

_____

_____

_____

Is there something you would like to let go of, such as resentment, anger or pride?

_____

_____

_____

_____

Self-Talk

*Thoughts of your mind have made you
what you are and thoughts of your mind
will make you what you become
from this day forward.*

Catherine Ponder

Before going any further into affirmations, it's important to take some time to become familiar with the term "self-talk." I use this term to describe the conversations we have in our minds, the words we say to ourselves. We constantly tell ourselves all kinds of things which we then internalize as truth. For example, a person with an eating problem might be 5' 4" tall and weigh 105 pounds and still tell herself she is too fat. A very competent person might not go for a job interview after convincing him or herself that he or she could not be hired.

It is crucially important to become aware of your self-talk if you hope to change it. Practice listening to the way you speak to yourself. Observe the effect that it has on your personal belief system.

Meditation is a wonderful technique for helping you to slow down and listen to your own thoughts. The practice of mindfulness, a form of meditation, not only helps you to increase your awareness of how you talk to yourself, but also helps you to stay in the present moment. I've written more about this in my other books.

Mindfulness is simply a quieting down of our mind, a settling down of our thoughts. Sitting quietly for only twenty minutes every morning, you begin to see how your mind works. By concentrating on your breathing, you'll see how your mind goes off in many other directions. Bring your attention back to your breathing. Every time your mind strays away, just notice it without any judgment and bring your attention back to your breathing. This practice helps you become aware of your self-talk. People who are just beginning this practice are often amazed at the language they use on themselves. They might discover themselves using abusive language such as, "Stupid! I should be able to stay with my breath." Many people have been talking to themselves like this for their entire lives, but have not been aware of it. They don't know that they are holding themselves back or keeping themselves in a state of low self-esteem.

Once we recognize and understand the power our thoughts have over our actions and feelings, we can learn to detach emotionally from them and observe them, sorting out the negative and destructive ones from the positive and constructive ones; realizing we do not have to believe them. These thoughts lose their power over us as soon as we become aware of them, because we can then choose to create more positive and constructive self-talk to inspire, encourage, affirm, accept, respect and love ourselves.

Remember:

- We are what we think about!
- What we think about expands.
- We feel what we think about.
- We create what we think about in our lives.

- When awareness increases, we draw to us what we think about.
- We attract what we think about.

The Power of Words

The word is not just a sound or a written symbol.
The word is a force, it is the power
you have to express and communicate,
to think, and thereby to create the events of your life.

Don Miguel Ruiz

Words are powerful! They have the power to move us. They can lift our spirits, inspire us, change our mood, give us courage, make us cry and do much more. They can move our life forward. As we become aware of our self-talk, the words that we say to ourselves, we can be mindful of the effect words have in our life. We will see how our mood can be changed by how we speak to ourselves, thus creating changes in the quality of our lives.

Our bodies do not know the difference between something real or something imagined. Our bodies respond to what we think about as if it were real. For example, think for a minute about something that makes you smile, or feel gentle or happy, such as a puppy, an ice cream cone or a sunset. Notice how these images make you feel. Now think about a time when you were fearful, and notice how those thoughts make you feel. Nothing will be changed in reality, but you will suddenly feel different. Words can block us from success or bring us success.

*Change the thought, change the feeling,
change the action.*

*Fear, for example, is only a thought
triggering a physical sensation.
Your word can create the most beautiful dream,
or your word can destroy everything around you.*

Don Miquel Ruiz

Negative Word Blockers That Keep Us from Moving Forward

When I say, "I can't," then I can't. I'll feel inadequate.

When I say, "I'll never be able to_____," then I never will be able to_____. I'll feel incapable.

When I say, "I haven't enough time," then I'm all about not having enough time. I'll feel rushed and full of anxiety.

Positive Word Releasers

When I say, "I AM TERRIFIC JUST THE WAY I AM!" I feel energized, enthused, upbeat.

When I say, "I AM FEELING PEACE IN THIS VERY MOMENT," I feel serene and peaceful.

When I say, "I HAVE ALL THE INTELLIGENCE I NEED TO PASS THIS TEST," I feel confident and strong.

2

The Power
of
Affirmations

*What we create within is mirrored
outside of us. That is the law of the universe.*

Shakti Gawain

When my first book, *The Journey Within: A Spiritual Path to Recovery,* was printed, Peter, my publisher, called to ask if I did public speaking. I said no. He asked if I would consider it, and I said no. He asked me to call him back in two weeks. I didn't. I was terrified of public speaking. I had some very embarrassing moments in school as a child and vowed I would never speak in front of people again. Peter called back in three weeks and told me I was on the agenda to speak in

Albany, New York, in October, three months away. I felt trapped, and I had three long months in front of me to feel my terror!

After listening to my negative self-talk, such as "I'm not good enough" and "Who would want to hear me speak?" for over two months, I remembered, fortunately, that affirmations work. I had been teaching affirmations in my meditation classes, yet my own fear blocked me from remembering to use them in this instance.

One important criteria for successful affirmations is to write each affirmation ten times a day for twenty-one consecutive days. By the time I remembered to use affirmations, it was only nineteen days before the conference. Could it work within the time left? I wrote the following affirmation ten times a day for nineteen days, hoping there would be enough time:

I am a dynamite, confident, fearless, charismatic and motivating speaker.

I didn't believe one word of it and was embarrassed to tell anyone my affirmation, but the power of those words carried me through that speaking engagement and hundreds of others since then. I soon became relaxed when speaking before an audience and now even enjoy it.

I've learned that the more we learn to quiet our minds and listen to our self-talk, the more we begin to discover that words have the power to make us feel good or bad, confident or fearful, positive or negative. It has been scientifically proven that the words we use can even make us healthy or sick.

Brain wave tests prove that when we use positive

words, our "feel good" hormones flow. Positive self-talk releases endorphins and serotonin in our brain, which then flow throughout our body, making us feel good. These neurotransmitters stop flowing when we use negative words.

We will have a new and extraordinarily effective technique for change when we realize that the way we feel can be a direct result of how we talk to ourselves. We do have a choice.

Affirmations are powerful tools for helping us break away from the way we normally think and talk to ourselves. By changing our thinking, we can change our attitude. By changing our attitude, we can change our energy. And by changing our energy, we can change our actions, and thus we change our lives.

Affirmations are so easy that some people think they are too simple to be effective. I have used them over and over and have taught them to thousands of people and the results have been amazing.

What Is an Affirmation?

Whether you think you can or can't, you're right!

Henry Ford

Affirmations are positive statements we say to ourselves. The definition of the word *affirm,* in *Funk & Wagnalls Standard College Dictionary,* is "to declare or state positively; assert and maintain to be true."

Five Parts to a Successful Affirmation

In order for an affirmation to be effective, I have found it must have each of the following characteristics:

1. **It Must Be Positive**

   Affirmations must be positive. If you want to be confident, for example, say, "I am confident today," not, "I am no longer negative."

2. **It Must Be Said and Felt with Passion and Power**

   When we state our affirmations with power and conviction, we begin the process of internalizing the positive statements that we tell ourselves. If we feel that what we tell ourselves is true in the present, we are opening our energies to accept our affirmation as true in the present.

   Affirmations must be said with positive feelings and with energy. They have to be stated so they are felt in your body. For example, if you are affirming that you feel good about yourself, imagine how your body would feel if you felt good and became aware of those bodily feelings.

   If you really do not believe what you are affirming, and you sincerely want it to be true, then give it "lip service." Act as if you believe it. If you "act as if" enough times, you will come to believe it to be true.

   As you say it with conviction, you are *energizing* your affirmation. Let yourself F E E E L your affirmation by actually visualizing it as real in the now. Let the good F E E E L I N G S pour through your body as you begin to reprogram yourself. Let yourself F E E E L the power of the words. For example:

"I am a confident person today."
Use the power of all your senses.

- *Think it.* You are recording your thoughts as you think them.
- *Feel it.* Write it or type it so you can feel it with your hands. Feel the pen or pencil or keyboard with your fingertips when you write it ten times a day for 21 days.
- *Hear it.* Say it aloud.
- *Smell it.* Be aware of the smell of the paper, the ink or the computer or typewriter.

3. **It Must Be Said in the Present Moment**
State affirmations as if they are happening and real *now.* Do not say this *will* happen because that is denying its existence in the now. By telling ourselves it is real *now,* it is becoming real in our subconscious. The subconscious does not know if something is happening in reality or happening in our minds.

We say, "I am confident TODAY," not, "I will be confident."

Our bodies do not know the difference between something real or imagined.

Our bodies respond to what we think about just as if it were actually happening.

4. **It Must Be Possible**
I cannot affirm that I am a famous singer, as I am tone deaf; but I can affirm that I am a successful writer.

5. **It Must Be Personal**
The affirmation must be personal. We can only affirm for ourselves. We must remember that we cannot change anyone else.

Repetition Is Important

Write Your Affirmation Ten Times a Day for 21 Consecutive Days

These five elements—positive, powerful, in the present, possible and personal—must be repeated. They work with repetition. Affirmations must be repeated for them to become a part of us. Countless experiments have proven that change occurs within 21 days when we repeat our affirmation at least ten times each day.

What We Think Is Best for Us Is Not Always Best for Us

It is not always true that we know what is best for ourselves, even though we think that when we get what, where or who we want we will be happy. When we learn to do the footwork, wait and listen, the right answer will always become apparent. Therefore, it is extremely important that while we are in the process of affirming what we want, we stay open to receiving what our Higher Power knows is really best for us. As Shakti Gawain says, "This or something better is manifesting itself for me."

Joan, wanting to make her ideas for children's mystery books a reality, began to seek publishers for them. She had taken my course in meditation and affirmations, and after a lot of thought, the one she chose to try was:

"I am making money through my writing."

She wrote it faithfully in her journal ten times every day for 21 days as she worked on her mystery book, filling notebooks with character sketches and bizarre plot twists.

Joan was also on the board of directors of her local library. The library, like so many other nonprofit institutions, was underfunded and the building was in need of repairs and painting. She decided to help by applying for a grant to cover refurbishing costs. During the 21-day affirmation period (while she contemplated what she would wear to her first children's-book signing), Joan wrote a grant that earned the library $25,000. This was enough for a complete inside and outside paint job. Not exactly what she had in mind with her affirmations, but, as she says, "Oh, so much better!"

Once you have created an affirmation or chosen one that fits you from the affirmation index, you now must write it ten times a day for 21 consecutive days. This is a critical component for success. Writing uses more of your senses. You are imprinting your affirmation deeply into your mind and your body.

Why 21 Days?

Many years ago, I read *Psycho-Cybernetics* by Maxwell Maltz, M.D. Dr. Maltz was a plastic surgeon who operated primarily on faces. He noticed, he said, a sudden and dramatic change in personality in most cases when he operated on "a person who had a conspicuously ugly face, or some 'freakish' feature. Usually there was a rise in self-esteem and self-confidence in 21 days. Those who didn't change continued to feel just as if they still had an ugly face."

Dr. Maltz wrote that it usually requires 21 days to affect any perceptible change, and he suggests reserving all

judgment for 21 days. When an arm or a leg is ampu-
tated, the "phantom limb" persists for about 21 days.
Though no one knows exactly why this number holds
such power over mind and body, Dr. Maltz and others
have observed this phenomena.

When I began practicing affirmations, I remembered
what Dr. Maltz wrote about 21 days, and I began to apply
his observation. I remember the time that I was involved
in starting Serenity House in Massachusetts, a halfway
house for women recovering from alcoholism. We desperately wanted to find the right house, raise the money,
acquire the town's approval and a contract with the state,
and so on. Finally, after a tremendous effort on the part
of a great many people, we accomplished enough of our
goals to move into the halfway house. I could not understand why I wasn't thrilled. I felt down, inexplicably, as if
there were something very wrong. It took me about three
weeks to feel at home and enjoy the hard-won accom-
plishment. Right on target, according to Dr. Maltz.

21 Days Means 21 Consecutive Days

We often begin a new project, such as writing affirmations, with great enthusiasm and energy. Perhaps we buy
a new notebook and place it just where we can see it
every day. Or we might carry it with us so we won't forget about our commitment.

Then the energy begins to wane, the enthusiasm begins
to slip away. This usually happens for me around the sixth
or seventh day. My fingers begin to cramp before I even
finish writing. My self-talk begins, such as "Is this really

going to work?" Am I holding my pen too tightly? I flex my fingers. Now 21 days seems like such a long time! I start thinking that I really don't have enough time and that I'll write the affirmation later. Soon, I forget, and I miss a day and need to start over. And then, maybe after only two or three days, I miss another one and I have to start over again. Once it took me six months to finish writing, "God is guiding the perfect person to us to buy our house today" ten times a day for 21 consecutive days. A purchase and sale agreement was signed just a few days after I finally completed 21 consecutive days.

Instant Affirmations

I can feel peace rather than this.

A Course in Miracles

While it can take 21 days to make changes in your life such as finding a new job, a home or a partner, or give up smoking or extra pounds, the good news is that you don't have to wait more than minutes to change how you feel in almost any given time. The power of words can be yours in an instant.

I missed an appointment one day by just a few minutes and was very upset with myself. I apologized to the woman and made another appointment. As I drove away, I became mindful of my self-talk and how I was verbally abusing myself with it.

"Jerk!" I heard myself saying. "Late again! Had to do that one more thing, didn't you?"

In the midst of this negative self-talk, I saw that my hand was suspended in mid-air, ready to slam down on the steering wheel in anger. I took a slow breath, and in a very gentle voice said out loud, "That's okay, Ruthie. (I notice that I call myself Ruthie when I'm being gentle with myself). You did the best you could. You'll see her on Friday."

A few minutes later I saw that I had subconsciously raised my hand again, and I slowly and consciously brought it back to the steering wheel, repeating to myself, "That's okay. Easy does it." This incident could have ruined my day if I allowed it. I chose peace instead.

As you become more and more aware of your self-talk, you will see that you have the power to change how you feel in an instant. Yelling at someone? Say STOP! to yourself, take a deep breath and calm down. In the middle of an interview or exam and feeling inadequate? Say, "I have all the skills I need to be hired for this job or pass this test."

Feeling negative? Think of the word NUTS, which stands for Negative and Unpleasant Thought Stopping. It's difficult to say NUTS without smiling, and it can quickly change your mood.

Full of fear? Take a deep breath and repeat the word faith, or power, or confidence.

Put soothing words in places where you might feel the most anxious.

Write the word peace on the top of a test.

Write the word peace on a scrap of paper and carry it with you in your pocket or purse. You'll know you have peace with you at all times.

Write easy does it on a piece of paper and paste it to the visor of your car.

Write I am full on a piece of paper and place it where

you can see it if you have a tendency to overeat.
Prone to losing your temper? Write *breathe* where you
can see it.

Where are you most vulnerable? Discover the words
that best work for you and practice using them. You'll be
amazed how quickly your feelings can change.

For a more lasting effect, use the 21-day plan to make
lifetime changes.

While this technique works very well for many situations, it is not a cure-all for severe emotional disturbances.
It does not take the place of counseling for more trau-
matic events in your life, but it does help.

Suggestions for Successful Affirmations: Simple Steps for Change

Create Your Intention

Decide what you would like to change. If you don't
have a specific change in mind, refer to the section on
"The place of not knowing."

Create Your Affirmation

Choose from more than 500 affirmations in this book
or write your own.

Follow Your Inner Voice

"What do you think of this," we might ask, holding our
breath for permission, approval or agreement.

"What do you think of that," we might question, wanting encouragement, help or advice.

There is nothing wrong with turning to others for

approval or advice, but you might not always get the positive feedback you seek. There might come a time when everyone with whom you speak says an emphatic "NO!", although you hear a "YES!" from within. There might come a time when we must follow our own "yes," even if it begins with only a whisper.

We must learn to follow our own path. We must listen to our own inner guidance, learning to trust that we know what is best for ourselves deep within, trusting our own intuition, listening to our own inner voice.

At times like this, you might want to use the following affirmation:

"Today I sit quietly, waiting to hear my intuitive voice, trusting the stirring and encouragement of my own inner wisdom."

Thaisa had developed what she called a 'compulsive' shopping behavior, and she became aware that shopping had become a negative pattern in her life. She had piles of shopping bags still unopened, even forgetting what she had purchased.

While it didn't put her in financial trouble, Thaisa wisely decided it was a conduct that was controlling her. Whenever she had inner feelings in conflict with each other, she would go shopping and come home distracted temporarily by her newest purchases. Needless to say, the feelings that she was trying to dispel were still there when she returned home.

She began asking herself what the real truth was underneath her compulsive shopping behavior. She soon discovered that it was her attempt to fill the lack of and longing for an active social and family life, and it was also a relief from stress. Having moved a continent away from them, Thaisa really missed her close friends and family ties.

I told Thaisa the story of the over-spender mentioned later in this book. Deciding to claim her power, Thaisa decided to try the same affirmation: *I have all that I need.* But, after a few tries, the words didn't feel right to her. She needed to choose the right words for herself, words that connected to her feelings and vibrations.

She chose:

"I find fulfillment in just _being_ today."

"That was exactly what my soul craved," she wrote. "By buying, I was choosing to 'have,' not to 'be.' The word 'being' played an important role in this affirmation. I knew that the key to any affirmation is to observe the feelings when we state them. My feelings needed to be in harmony with my words. Did I feel good in just being? Was it really possible to find fulfillment in just being? My answer was YES. That meant what I stated in the affirmation was not only possible and positive, in the present moment, but most important it made me feel good and motivated me toward my ultimate goal, to change my shopping behavior. I believed in what my affirmation said. Consequently, it felt right and had a good vibration. So I wrote that affirmation for 21 days.

"Today, I believe I am healed. I am not saying I do not shop anymore. Who doesn't? I am stating that when I have an inner feeling of dissatisfaction, I just become aware of it and look for 'being' alternatives to find fulfillment in life. After all, nobody ever found permanent happiness in life by having. Happiness is only found by being and giving. It gave me a tremendous sense of freedom and peace to know that I am in charge of my life."

Speak Softly and Slowly

Say the words softly and slowly to yourself. Your breath will slow down and deepen. The pause between your in breath and your out breath will increase. You might even feel as if time is standing still.

Visualize the Results

> Have in mind the great image
> and the empire will come to you.
>
> Lao-tzu, Tao Te Ching

Don't wait for your intention to come true. Don't even wait until you believe it will come true. Visualize it now, as if it were true in the present moment.

Whether or not we are aware of it, a thought always precedes an action. It's an automatic response. In addition, our body doesn't know the difference between something real or imagined.

For example, imagine an ice cream cone in just the flavor you love the most. If you don't like ice cream, imagine a special treat, a favorite food. Picture it with all the details you can remember. Its color, size, shape, texture and odor. Most likely you can feel your mouth watering!

To show how real your imagination can make things seem, imagine you are sauntering in the woods on a lovely day. Suddenly, you hear a noise and you look up and a huge black bear is coming toward you. What do you feel?

The more we imagine the results of our desires, our bodies remember the image and respond to it. So create a good picture in your mind of how you will look when your intention becomes real. Begin with the overall image. Then let yourself feeel what you think it would be like to have this desire be a reality in your life. Visualize it before writing your affirmations each day.

Let Go of Details

It's better not to imagine all the details of your intention. For example, let's say you would like to have a flower shop in a particular neighborhood. You're absolutely sure that you want it there, and you won't settle for anything less. You visualize it on a busy road with a traffic light on the corner so that people will have to stop and notice you! You imagine at least two greenhouses and a large parking lot. You may have to wait for years for such an opportunity to be available.

Imagine instead an attractive flower shop in a nice neighborhood where people would otherwise need to travel for miles to buy plants, flowers and all their garden needs.

Know that the right shop with the perfect rent for your budget is in the picture. Know that all the details will fall into place in the right time for you. And know that if this is God's will for you, it will happen in God's time.

Your affirmation might be:

I am being led on the right path for me today, leaving all the details to God.

FEEEL Your Words

Feel for yourself how words can change how you feel and move you toward deeper change. Remember that the words that we say to ourselves change how we feel.

I was still involved with the development of SpiritLifters, my new line of greeting cards, when at the same time, I had a deadline of August to finish this book. The greeting cards involved so many details. Every day I would tell myself that I would spend more time writing the book, but every day I would put it off for tomorrow. I rationalized by thinking I would finish this one more detail and then that one more thing, and on, and on, and on.

One day I realized I had to get serious and let go and just finish the book.

I said to myself, *I am excited about writing this book.*

I feeel excitement pouring through me as I think about writing my book!

I am making time today to write my book.

I felt stimulated. I felt energy pouring down my arms.

I actually felt my body moving forward although I actually was standing still. Remember, positive self-talk releases endorphins and serotonin in our brain, which then flow throughout our body, making us feel good. They stop flowing when we use negative words.

Try it out when you write your affirmation.

I am excited about _____.

I feeel excitement pouring through me as I think about

_____.

I am making time today to _____.

Keep a Separate Notebook

Use it only for your affirmations. Keep this notebook in the same place all the time. If you are a daily meditator, it is a good idea to keep it where you meditate. Then you can get into a routine and do one routine after the other. Keeping the notebook on a table next to your bed will help you remember when you wake up or before you go to sleep.

I've found that when I use the notebook that includes other things as well, such as my "to do" list or other writing ideas, it can end up on my desk in another room, or in a bag I carry to teach meditation or put on a workshop. I have skipped many a day because the book wasn't where I could see it to remind me to write, causing me to start over again and again. When the notebook is next to my bed in clear view, I don't miss a day.

Use Your Computer

It's okay to type affirmations into your computer as long as you actually type the sentences out ten times each day. This can save your fingers from cramping. You will also know that you have your affirmation saved in one place.

Dittos don't count!

Use Reminders

If you are writing your affirmation in your computer, it's helpful to place a sticky note right on the frame of your monitor so you will see it every day. It also helps to write your affirmation as soon as you sit down at your computer, because if you do something else first, the note often blends into the furniture. You'll no longer be aware of it and you might miss the day and have to start over again. Your computer calendar can also be set to pop up every day to remind you to write your affirmation.

Remember, the affirmation needs to be written for 21 consecutive days. Therefore do anything you can to help you remember to write it. You can place a reminder on your bathroom mirror, on a file card for your purse or pocket, on the visor of your car or on your refrigerator.

Begin with Gratitude

It is a good idea to list some things you are grateful for before beginning a new affirmation. As Sharon Anderson writes in *The Universal Spiritual Laws:* "If you're not grateful for what you already have, why should the Universe give you more?"

Use One Primary Affirmation at a Time

I am often asked if it is all right to write more than one affirmation at a time. Yes, you can. But, choose one to be your primary affirmation. This way, if you are unable to continue writing more than one, you can maintain the most important one until the 21 days are completed. Later, you can go on to do another one.

Listen to Your Self-Talk

As you go through your day, notice that negative, limiting thoughts are in direct or indirect opposition to reaching your goal. It can be as direct as *I'll never make it. I'm not smart enough*, or so indirect that you can barely notice it, such as *Now there's a smart dresser!* In this case, you might not be aware that you're really putting yourself down.

Become Aware of Your Judgments

Notice your likes, dislikes and opinions. Don't judge yourself for having them. Simply raise your awareness of them. You can go to the index and find judgments and choose one of the affirmations to use to let them go.

Write Down Your Limiting Thoughts

Take some time to write down the blocks that keep you stuck. As you listen to your self-talk and watch your negative thinking, write everything down without any judgment. Accept them as a part of you, not all of you.

The more you become tuned into the thoughts that keep you stuck, the more quickly you will be able to let them go.

Begin to Connect Your Thoughts to Your Feelings

Notice how positive thoughts connect with pleasant feelings while negative thoughts make you feel tense, angry, unhappy or depressed. You will soon increase your ability to be aware of how your thoughts affect your moods and your actions. You will see how these words have the power to make you feel good or bad, confident or fearful, positive or negative. It has been scientifically proven that the words we use in our self-talk can heal us or make us sick. Remember that it has been proven that positive words increase the flow of our endorphins, our feel-good hormones, thus making us feel better. Negative thoughts block our endorphins and can lead to depression.

Change How You Talk to Yourself

Once we realize that the way we feel is a direct result of how we talk to ourselves, then we have a new and powerful tool to change our feelings. We have a choice.

There's a wonderful Sioux Indian story about how our thoughts not only create our own feelings but affect the feelings of others.

My grandfather took me to the fish pond on the farm when I was about seven, and he told me to throw a stone into the water. He told me to watch the circles created by the stone. Then he asked me to think of myself as that stone person. You may create lots of splashes in your life but the waves that come from those splashes will disturb the peace of all your fellow creatures, he said.

Remember that you are responsible for what you put in your circle because that circle will also touch many other circles. You will need to live in a way that allows the good that comes from your circle to send the peace of that goodness to others. The splash that comes from anger or jealousy will also send those feelings to other circles. You are responsible for both.

That was the first time I realized each person creates the inner peace or discord that flows out into the world. We cannot create world peace if we are riddled with inner conflict, hatred, doubt or anger. We radiate the feelings and thoughts that we hold inside, whether we speak them or not. Whatever is splashing around inside of us is spilling out into the world, creating beauty or discord with all other circles of life. Remember the eternal wisdom: whatever you focus on expands.

Turn Around Your "I Can't Because . . ."

Soon you'll begin to know how your I can'ts really hold you back. For example, change "I can't get into college because I'm not smart enough," to "I'm smart enough to get into just the right college for me." Change "I can't lose weight because I've tried it before and it never lasts," to "I'm moving toward the perfect weight for me today." You get the idea! Trust that the universe will provide you with the perfect college, the perfect weight, the perfect relationship. You simply need to provide the willingness and the intention to follow where it leads.

Take One Step at a Time

Many years ago, I attended EST, a personal training seminar. We were taught a simple lesson that has stayed with me over the years. The trainer asked us to turn and look at a door in the back of the room. He then stated an obvious fact. "No matter how much you want to be at that door, you can't just be at that door. You can only get there one step at a time."

Alcoholics Anonymous teaches the same message. Alcoholics don't have to imagine not drinking for the rest of their lives. They just have to stay sober one day at a time.

In this age of fast food, instant messages and wireless phones, we have come to expect everything to happen right now. We want success, fame, money and everything else immediately.

If we don't have instant gratification, we become frustrated and impatient.

You Have to Do the Footwork

Knowledge without action
is the greatest self-con of all.

Sharon Wegscheider-Cruse

Relationships can improve through changes in our attitude. Our attitudes will improve if we write ten times a day consistently for 21 days. As long as we are willing to change and make an intention for it to occur, change will happen. Negative feelings can be released when we focus on positive affirmations, thus reducing and eliminating barriers between ourselves and others.

Still, we must realize that affirmations aren't magic. Our dreams aren't necessarily going to suddenly manifest into our lives just because we write them ten times a day for 21 days. Many affirmations require more effort on our parts. A new job won't come to us just because we have affirmed that we are getting one and then only stay home and watch television. We might have to do research to find the appropriate companies, write a good résumé and perhaps, even buy a new outfit to wear to go on job interviews.

If we want a new relationship, we can't simply sit in our living rooms and wait for the phone or doorbell to ring. Although the person who delivers the mail might be just the person we want to be with for the rest of our lives, most likely we have to go to places where single people meet or join a group or club or organization. We must make ourselves available. We must be open to what is out there waiting to come into our lives. We must open the door if we want to receive what is on the other side.

Our affirmations create positive energy and help us to be open to positive change. Father Martin, a well-known speaker in recovery circles, gives us this wonderful example:

"There was a young woman who wanted to be a doctor. Every night she prayed and prayed that God would make her a doctor. After ten years of praying with nothing happening, she asked God why he didn't help her become a doctor. Suddenly, she heard a voice. It said, 'Go to medical school!'"

Another wonderful example is a Sufi story adapted by Anthony de Mello:

"A man walked through the forest and saw a fox that had lost its legs and wondered how it lived. Then he saw a tiger come up with game in its mouth. The tiger ate its fill and left the rest of the meat for the fox.

"The next day God fed the fox by means of the same tiger. The man began to wonder at God's greatness and said to himself, 'I too shall just rest in the corner with full

trust in the Lord and he will provide me with all that I need.'
"He did this for many days but nothing happened. He
was almost at death's door when he heard a voice say,
'Oh, you who are on the path of error, open your eyes to
the truth! Stop imitating the disabled fox and follow the
example of the tiger.'"

We Don't Always Get What We Want

Shakti Gawain, author of *Creative Visualizations,*
wrote that when completing an affirmation, know or say
"This or something better for all concerned is manifesting
itself for me." It is not always true that we know what is
best for ourselves, and if we learn to wait and listen, the
right answer will be there.

God Might Have a Better Plan

Sometimes you get what you need,
even when you don't ask for it!

Author Unknown

Because she had low self-esteem, Heather had trouble
believing that she could accomplish anything. When I met
her, she was feeling down and discouraged, yet willing to
try an affirmation. I suggested she use "I believe in myself
today."

After only four days, she stopped smoking, even
though the affirmation was not aimed at helping her to
stop smoking. Actually, she had wanted to stop smoking
for some time, but had never believed she could really do
it. Then she started writing my suggested affirmation and
suddenly decided to quit smoking cold turkey. She hasn't
had a cigarette since.

Removing the Barriers to Change

Re-examine all you have been told.
Dismiss what insults your soul.

Fear

You might think that if you are hired for a new job, you won't be capable of handling the responsibilities that come with it. Or perhaps you are afraid that the person who didn't get the job will feel discouraged, or, even worse, be upset with you or dislike you. Fear has been described as:

False
Evidence
Appearing
Real

If you worry or have fear, you are not living in the present moment. You're in the future, creating a scenario straight from your imagination, colored by your feeling in the present moment.

Walking Through Our Fears

There is nothing more difficult to take in hand,
more perilous to conduct, or more uncertain
in its success, than to take the lead in
the introduction of a new order of things.

Niccolo Machiavelli, *The Prince*

Going off into an unknown territory, whether it be to change the world, our jobs, our relationships or our attitudes, can cause us tremendous fear and anxiety. Going off into the unknown at any level can reproduce all our old insecurities, plus bring us some new ones. Today's fear can trigger yesterday's fears, which can trigger earlier fears, and so on, until what we are actually feeling can be so voluminous that it will feel as if the change is far beyond our ability to manage.

Just the consideration of change can result in anxiety and stress, leading to a shutting down of our motivation or a rushing forward to get the change over with right away.

If we can accept that some tension, stress, anxiety and fear are to be expected, and often come with the territory of the unknown, then we can learn to be with these feelings and accept them as a normal part of life. Know that fear is normal. Remember,

Courage is fear that has said its prayers.

Know that we have choices today. We can stay where we are and do nothing, putting up with unacceptable conditions. Or we can take a chance and begin to change the things that are not working in our lives, knowing that is the only way to grow.

Ask yourself questions such as:

Is the risk of staying still and doing nothing greater than the risk of change?

What is doing nothing about an unacceptable situation doing to me mentally, spiritually and physically?

Can I honestly justify the comfort of the known, even when it is obviously damaging, versus the anxiety I might feel with the unknown results of change?

You need to ask yourself questions such as these before you can decide what to do. When you come to questions which you can't answer, try the Serenity Prayer:

> God, grant me the serenity
> To accept the things I cannot change,
> The Courage to change the things I can
> And the wisdom to know the difference.

An affirmation that you might want to do to help walk through your fear:

> "I am not letting my fears stop me from making healthy changes in my life."

Self-Limiting Thoughts

Thoughts such as, "I'm not good enough," or "I'll never pass this exam," or "I'll never be hired for that job," keep us from moving forward.

As I wrote earlier, I love convertibles. Ever since I was in college I've had a convertible. In my years without much money, my convertibles were old. Later, I was able to afford newer ones. The only time I did not have a convertible in my life was during the first ten years that I co-founded and co-directed Serenity House.

A small grant from the state covered only a portion of our expenses and in order to make ends meet we were dependent on outside donations. People who believed in our cause donated money, sometimes when they barely had enough money of their own. I remember a blind woman once saved $6 and donated it to us. Churches raised money through bake sales.

One of the fringe benefits in lieu of a decent salary was that I did have the use of a company car. I bought one of the least expensive cars on the market. My thoughts were that if I bought a convertible, people would think I was using donated money frivolously and would stop making donations. But, oh, how I longed for a convertible.

Thinking about this one day, I realized that I had never done an affirmation around having a convertible. People I knew were getting new jobs, new relationships and much more as I drove in a car that blocked me from the joy of feeling the breeze in my hair and the sun on my face. I decided I would write an affirmation. So I began, "I deserve a convertible." I had only written the affirmation for four days when a friend said she received a call from another friend who saw a convertible for sale in a parking lot near her home. As I rushed over to look at it, a light went on in my mind. It was a 1969 Mustang. The year this happened for me was 1986. The car was seventeen years old. It was too new to be a classic or worth much money, but it had been well cared for by the people who loved it.

It had never occurred to me to be looking for an older convertible. My mind had been closed, stuck in the idea of "what would people think" if I drove around in a convertible. I assumed people would judge it to be a flashy, extravagant and expensive car.

I called the number printed on the windshield and was delighted to hear that the price was only $3,100; and yes, I could have the car checked out by my mechanic. In a few days, I felt as if I were in heaven, driving guilt free, one with the wind and sun, in a car I paid for by myself.

My old "what would people think" tapes had kept me from something that gave me a great deal of enjoyment. My self-talk produced the fear that if people didn't approve of what I was doing, they wouldn't give us any more donations.

If you play the same CD over and over again,
you're going to hear the same music!

R.F.

Worry

Worry is similar to fear. Worry thoughts go round and round in our minds, drain our energy and leave us depressed and uninspired. Affirmations are an excellent way to get rid of worry and fear thoughts.

Focusing on What You Don't Want

Our focus is often on thoughts such as not wanting to struggle, or be fat, or live alone and so forth. When we think of what we don't want, we are putting a negative message out into the universe. The universe hears struggle, stress, fat, or live alone, etc.

A good way to turn this around is to make a list of what you don't want and turn them around to your wants. For example, if you don't want to be fat, think thin instead. If you don't want to feel stress, think relax. If you don't want financial insecurity, think prosperity.

The Place of Not Knowing

What if you're miserable but don't know what to change? Sometimes the need to make a particular change shouts at you so loudly you can't ignore it. If you're miserable in your job, it's obviously time to find a new one. If you're 60 pounds overweight and have a heart problem, it's obviously time to change your eating habits. If you've carried a resentment against someone the last seven years and finally see that it is hurting you more than the other person, it's obviously time to practice forgiveness.

But what can you do if you're just plain unhappy and don't have a clue about what to change? You might try some affirmations from faith such as:

"All the answers I need are coming to me as I need them."

or from purpose:

"I am waiting patiently for clarification of my purpose."

The Place of In-Between

What if you are at a crossroad in your life? Perhaps you are close to graduating from high school and you don't know whether to get a job, join the military or go to college.

In all of these situations you might consider affirmations for faith such as:

"I am open to what God wants for me. All the energies of the universe are guiding me to my next step."

If you're open to what the universe has to offer you, your next step could turn out to be a complete surprise. Perhaps you'll start your own business, or inherit a fortune so that you can travel for a year.

Faith affirmations can be a great comfort in this place in-between, this place of not knowing, which can be so very stressful. How well I remember sending out book proposals and waiting to hear from an editor, not knowing whether to continue writing or take up another line of work. Affirmations such as:

*"All the answers I need are coming to me
as I need them."*
*"Today I trust I will have my answers in
the right time."*

helped me get through these frustrating times.

Meditation and guided imageries are also good techniques to use when going through these periods of fear,
doubt and insecurity. Prayer is talking to God, and meditation is listening. Meditation is simply quieting your mind,
settling down your thoughts, stopping your inner clutter.

There are hundreds of books and tapes on meditation.
I have written extensively about it in my books. I won't go
into it much more here except to say that meditation is
very helpful in deepening our spirituality, connecting with
our own inner voice, learning to listen to our self-talk and
living a less stressful, healthier and happier life.

Guided imageries consist of allowing someone else's
voice to guide our imagination to take us to a deeper level
of consciousness, a place where we can connect symbol-
ically with our wise self. By meditating first to quiet your
mind and then finding a special place inside, you can ask
your Higher Power or your wise self for guidance. With
practice you can come to a place of inner knowing, learning to trust your intuition. Affirmations such as: *I am
learning to trust my inner voice* have been helpful to
many people.

Not Really Being Willing

I have lived with clutter in my office and wherever else I work ever since I can remember. Within a half hour into speaking at a conference or workshop, I can look down and see my papers scattered here and there. I recreate my work environment wherever I am! I remember as clearly as yesterday walking through Harvard Square in Cambridge, Massachusetts, the year after I graduated from college and seeing a plaque in a store window jump out at me: *"Tomorrow I'm going to get organized!"*

Yes! I said to myself, and went into the store to buy the plaque. I have carried it with me everywhere I have moved since that day and have hung it in every office I have been in where I can easily see it.

I am actually very organized when it comes to a specific project I am working on, such as when I am writing a book or preparing for a workshop. My bills are all in one place, as are many of the other projects I might work on at one time or another. But there is still a large pile of paper scattered everywhere. Recently a friend suggested that I have been putting out the word tomorrow into the universe, rather than "I am getting organized today" or "I am an organized person." I might try that . . . tomorrow!

As you'll see on the next section on prefaces, I can affirm, "I'm willing to be willing to be more organized," or, "I'm willing to move toward being a more organized person." Then, when my willingness increases, I can affirm, "I'm an organized person today!"

Prefaces

Sometimes, even when we see the advantages of making a specific change, we just aren't ready to make it. Early in my recovery, I had a very difficult time staying sober. I was lost in the paradox of wanting to feel better but not committed enough to go through the suffering required to stopping drinking. In fact, I could not imagine going through twenty-four hours without a drink. Someone suggested that I pray for the willingness to be willing to stop. Finally it worked! Very gradually I became willing to be willing, and finally became willing to stop. At the time of this writing, I have stopped for almost twenty-nine years.

Unwillingness to forgive is another example of not being ready, even when we know it is for our own good. Forgiveness can be very difficult for many of us. We might know rationally that it is healthy to forgive, but emotionally we might not want or be ready to let go of our resentments. Our anger might be so great that the very idea of forgiving someone who did something to us can be impossible even to imagine. We can feel completely justified in holding on to our resentments. *Look what he did to me,* we might think, or, *After all she put me through? No way!*

It has been said that holding on to one's resentments is like drinking arsenic and expecting the other person to die. Or, like holding a burning coal in one hand waiting for the perfect time to throw it at someone, while it burns our own hand in the process.

We need to look at who we are really hurting.

While knowing that we forgive for our own good, the preface "becoming willing" is very helpful. It is also helpful to ask for help from a Power greater than ourselves. It is a relief when you know that through faith and prayer you are not alone and can receive help making your changes. One affirmation that is very effective to begin the process on forgiveness is: *God is helping me to become willing to forgive*_____. After 21 days of writing this, now write *I am becoming willing to forgive* _____, and then after 21 more days, *I am forgiving* _____. It might take 63 days for this one, but each step is a process that can move us forward. The freedom felt when we finish is well worth the struggle.

One of the miracles about willingness to forgive is that we may be completely amazed at how quickly the process goes once we have made a beginning. Sometimes we see that our barriers disappear quickly once we start to take them down. The freedom that takes their place can be extremely rewarding.

More Preparation Prefaces

Before saying, "No, I'm not ready to give this up," or, "I can't give this up," try a preface to get ready. This prepares you to be willing to do something in the future, but doesn't put pressure on you in the present moment. For example, try:

"I'm becoming willing to be a non-smoker," or
"I'm in the process of becoming a non-smoker," or even
"I'm becoming willing to become willing to be willing to become a non-smoker." This really puts it off!
Another preface is:

"I'm learning how to study to get better grades." Here

again, you're not quite there yet to put the effort into doing the work, but you're getting ready.

"I intend . . ."

"I trust . . ."

"I'm in the process of . . ."

"It feeels so good to . . ."

This is especially good if you are feeling any anger, fear, hesitation or other uncomfortable feelings. For example, you might have a job interview and might hear a lot of negative self-talk. "I know I'll never get this job." You begin to feel sick to your stomach just thinking about the interview. When you affirm, "It feeels so good to know that I am an excellent candidate for this job," your feeling changes. You'll become aware of buoying energy pouring through your body. Remember, your self-talk depletes your energy. Positive words stimulate it.

Monkey Mind

Our minds have been compared to monkeys, jumping from branch to branch going wherever they want to go. Writing affirmations helps us to focus, to keep our mind where we want it to be and not jumping everywhere it wants to go.

If we don't let go, we can't move forward.

R.F.

If you are regretful about the past or worrying about the future, your energy is stuck and you can't move forward.

Thinking You Have to Do Everything Yourself

Whether you believe in God or not, be aware that more exists than we know of in our world. So much is a mystery. We didn't create the universe. A Power beyond us did. When we allow ourselves to open to Universal Energy, when we let a Higher Power be in charge of our lives, we can relax and go with the flow. And as we relax and give up our fears and doubts, our tension and resistance, change begins to take place. Miracles begin to happen. Life becomes so much easier.

Very Personal

I have varied the use of the word God, Higher Power or Universal Energy in different affirmations. Other times I have left out any mention of a Power Greater than Ourselves entirely. Use any word that feels right to you. You can use God, Higher Power, All the energies of the Universe, Spirit, Allah, Jesus Christ, Moses, Universal Energy, Angels, Spirit Guides, or Jehovah and others. Choose one or choose not to use any. Design your affirmation to be as personal to you as you can. For example,

"God is guiding me to the perfect job for me today."
"I am finding the perfect job for me today."

The most important thing is that you feel comfortable with the words you will be living with for 21 days.

Goals and Dreams
Versus Living in the Now

It's important to know that you don't have to wait for the results of your affirmations to transpire before you can be happy. Many people think that they can only be happy when or if things change. They think, "If I could just block this pain I would be happy," or, "When I get a new job, my life will be better," or, "When I hit the lottery," or, "Move to Cape Cod," or, "Move away from Cape Cod," my life will be complete. Some of us think happiness lies outside of ourselves, when it really lies within us.

This present moment leads us into the next moment and into the next moment. When we can stay in the present moment, life naturally moves us forward. This is the way of life. Spring moves into summer, moves into fall, moves into winter and moves into spring again. When we follow our inner spirit and let our soul direct our course, our lives flow.

What does "being fully alive in the present moment" mean? And how do we get there? Living in the present moment simply means being free to be with whatever is going on in your life now, without wishing it to be different. It means not letting yourself be blocked by feelings of anger, resentment, guilt or shame from the past, or fears of the future. It means letting go of judgments and opinions and simply accepting what is right now and right now and right now. . . .

It also means growth and change. Our natural inclination is to grow and change, wish and want. Human beings are constantly evolving. This seems to be in conflict with accepting what is right now. How can we evolve and still be in the now? And why use affirmations to change if we want to learn to be content and accept the moment?

While our intention is to find peace in the moment, to be okay in this moment, it does not mean that we have to stay in unhealthy, unpleasant conditions. For example, the job you are in might be very stressful or even abusive, so you have decided to leave and find a new job. You might have to stay in your old job a bit longer because you can't afford to leave before you have the new job. You need your weekly salary. However, affirmations can help you be peaceful with your decision to leave. You can use affirmations such as "God is guiding me toward the perfect job for me" or "I am discovering the perfect job for me today." We still can have our goals and dreams, but we don't need to reach them in order to feel peace and contentment. We can be content in the knowledge that we are moving toward them.

Perhaps our lives are positive and full and there isn't anything we want to change. We can still grow and learn while we are content and grateful for what we have in our lives. We can use:

"I'm growing spiritually."
"God is guiding me to my next step."

There are so many things that block us from letting our soul direct our path. Here, too, is where our affirmations can help. Affirmations take us by the hand and help us step over a barrier or climb over a wall or move away a rock or a stick. Affirmations make it possible to change the negative thinking that keeps us stuck, to rewire the circuitry in our brain. Affirmations help us direct our thoughts to a Higher Power, giving the energy in the universe permission to flow through us. Affirmations help us to clarify our dreams, expand and raise our consciousness, and let our hearts stretch open and fill with love.

Learning to Stay in the Present Moment

You can't make anything happen if you're wasting your energy regretting the past or living in fear of the future. You can only move forward when you are focused in the present moment.

A good technique to help you become aware of how much you are in the past or in the future is to watch what happens to your mind when you are doing something routine, like taking a shower or brushing your teeth. Notice how often you are into planning, thinking, regretting, daydreaming or worrying.

A great way to practice staying in the present moment is to take that time in the shower or brushing your teeth and bring your full awareness to all your senses that are involved:

- Feel the water on your body or in your mouth.
- Feel the texture of the soap or the toothbrush in your hand.
- Listen to the sound of the toothbrush against your teeth and gums.
- Hear the water as it pours from the faucet.
- Smell the soap and the toothpaste.
- Observe all the details of where you are and what you are doing.

Umbrella Affirmations

When the songs of your heart start singing,
you should gratefully listen . . . for the harmony
is that which will bring you happiness
and the melody is the voice of your true spirit.

Author Unknown

Not all affirmations have to be specifically focused on one goal. There are times when it appears that you need to use two or three affirmations to make a change. Try, instead, to combine them into one. I planned a wonderful trip to Florida and back in February 2002, fully intending to spend lots of time in the sun. As an author, I had a perfect way of combining business and pleasure. I set up book signings and workshops up and down the East Coast and in Florida. There were incredible details to coordinate to make a trip like this happen. Timing and mileage were crucial. Contacting the appropriate person in the bookstore could take days, demanding a large part of my time for months to put it all together.

Around three weeks before my departure date, when there were still a great many details to take care of, ideas for greeting cards suddenly began popping into my head. I began to get excited, thinking that this would be a wonderful addition to sell along the way to help pay for this trip. I had been in the greeting card business years earlier and therefore knew how to make it happen again.

Thinking I would begin with a few cards, and that I would spend just a few hours on each one, I began the process of learning how to create them on my computer. Scanning-in actual art work from my books was easy. But teaching myself how to color them was a different story. My "few hours on each one" turned into days—and the ideas kept coming.

I began to think something was wrong with me. Was I procrastinating? I knew I hated details. Was this just a diversion, an extreme game of avoidance? I created and created and created, forcing myself to stop to make calls that were necessary for the trip. I was convinced something was wrong with me. Soon, I had created nine greeting cards, ordered envelopes, and spent hours going back and forth to the printer. I was deeply into my creativity and loving it, filled with joy and excitement.

The only deterrent to this wonderful state was the nagging thought that something was wrong with me. Was I wasting my time? Were my mind, talents and energy being drained?

I decided to write an affirmation to help me through my doubts, an affirmation that would include all the aspects I was concerned about.

I began writing:

> "God is guiding me in the perfect use of my mind, time, gifts and energy."

It worked! From past experience, I know that when I follow my inner voice, I am doing what I was meant to be doing. I began to trust that I would have time to do everything that was necessary for my trip and continued to work on the creation of SpiritLifters, as I called them. Three days before our departure, I forced myself to stop where I was in the greeting card process. I did have all the time I needed to do what needed to be done. And the greeting cards were well received, a great success!

When Not to Think About Making Changes

There are times when it is not in our best interests even to consider changing anything. There are times when staying right where we are is exactly where we belong. Here are a few examples:

Grief

When we experience a loss of any kind, whether it be from a job, friendship or death of a loved one, it is important that we don't hide from those feelings or feel as if we have to rush through them and move on. Some people try to bury the pain from loss by the use of drugs, alcohol, food or other stimulants such as gambling or shopping. Any kind of overconsuming may make you feel better for the moment, but sooner or later you will have to deal with the feelings if you are to remain healthy and eventually move your life forward.

There are many ways to move through grief. Talking about your feelings to a friend or therapist is one of the most helpful ways. Writing, when talking about them is too difficult or impossible, helps to keep the feelings from being stuck inside. Praying and meditating, taking time with nature and joining a support group, all help us to pass through these types of difficult times.

Affirmations can help. Look in chapter 6 for *difficult situations, faith, grief* and *healing*.

Stuck in the Past

There are times in our lives when we must stop and do some serious soul searching. Sometimes exploring our history is important. We can't go forward fully until we look at our past and make peace with it. We might need to let go of old anger and resentments. We can't move forward until we become willing to forgive ourselves and others. We have to give up alcohol or drugs or other addictions so we can be fully present in each moment. We need to let go of feelings of victimization or self-pity.

Twelve-step programs have a technique that can be used by anyone. They suggest taking a personal inventory of the exact nature of the wrongs we have done to others and then talking about them to God and another human being. This process helps to release anger, resentments and any guilt and shame we might be holding on to from the past. Done faithfully, real life changes occur.

Look in chapter 6 for *acceptance, letting go* or *forgiveness.*

Healing

Sometimes we just need to stop and rest and heal, such as after an operation or a huge disappointment.

Look in the index for *healing, health, meditation* or *miracles.*

Slowing Down and Resting

Perhaps you have just put a tremendous amount of energy into a massive project, such as studying for the bar exam or doing a science project. It might be time to simply slow down, rest and take some time off before even thinking about moving forward.

Look in chapter 6 for *meditation, time* or *solitude.*

Time Out

It's important to have balance in our lives. Take a vacation, go on a retreat or just do absolutely nothing! Stop and have fun!

Look in chapter 6 for *fun, peace* or *relaxation.*

Yes, They Work!

Over the years, many people have shared their successful experiences with affirmations with me. The following are a just few. May they inspire you to wonderful changes!

A Cancer Survivor of Many Years

Margie Levine is the bestselling author of *Surviving Cancer*, which was nominated by the NAPA as one of the four best health books in the country. She is a wonderful example of how visualizations work together with affirmations to create miracles.

Margie has survived mesothelioma, the rarest and most aggressive form of lung cancer. She told me that affirmations played a huge role in her recovery. Margie Levine has been a health education coordinator in a public school, a social worker, and a therapist who specialized in integrative medicine. Her book *Surviving Cancer* is the result of her belief that she is alive today for a reason.

With all the knowledge she had from her professional experience, she was able to put together a personal program for healing that saved her life. She continues to reach out to others who embrace health challenges.

"Repeating reinforcing thoughts helped me to heal mentally, physically and spiritually. I created my own tape using my voice. Hearing my own voice was magical, as I gave direction to my body cells. I affirmed that the cancer cells were leaving my lungs through my skin pores. I confirmed that I was getting stronger every day. I then worked with my fear and repeated that it was being swept from my body with huge straw brooms, just as I visualized it happening in my mind's eye. I repeated these thoughts many times. Then I put Mozart music in the background and listened to it daily. My affirmation tape was the last thing I heard before being wheeled to surgery each time.

"I learned to apply 'affirmations on demand.' Laying scrunched in the narrow MRI machines listening to the loud banging in my ear, I visualized hovering angels with axes hammering away at my tumor. At the same time I affirmed out loud that the cancerous growth was shrinking. I repeated, 'I will be strong. I will survive!'

"When I was wheeled out by the techs, I was 'high' on my body's own endorphins.

"Affirmations played a vital role in my healing. Words have power. Positive thoughts can shift energy and help heal disease."

Triumphing Over Her Weight

Karen sent in this success story:

> "At one time I weighed 194 pounds. I had read about affirmations, that the subconscious could not discern between truth or fiction and that whatever you told yourself, and believed, would be who you became. I had become an overweight woman. After all, I wasn't meant to be thin, according to an old family belief. I was thrilled to learn on the day that I read about affirmations that I could create new weight and body-type affirmations to literally change and transform my body and my mind.

These are the affirmations I wrote:

> 'I weigh 145 pounds and I always have enough time, energy and desire to exercise my body.'
> 'I weigh 145 pounds and I have created my perfect body with slim, trim limbs and firm toned muscle.'
> 'I weigh 145 pounds and I maintain my weight easily, as I only eat foods that are healthy and consistent with a slim, trim figure.'
> 'Nothing tastes as good as thin feels.'

"It has worked for a long time. I weighed between 140 to 145 for fifteen years! I now weigh 160 and need to use my affirmations again."

They Work Even if We Don't Follow All the Directions!

Dale's lease was up and she had no place to go. Her landlady wanted her out in one month. When I met her, she told me her funds were limited and she was beginning to panic. I suggested a few affirmations she might try. One was:

> *"I am finding the right place to be safe, happy and secure."*

She forgot about the fact that one of the five important parts of an affirmation is that it must be stated in the present. When you use will it is always in the future.

She wrote:

> *"I will be open to my Higher Power's plan for me about where to live."*
> *"I will find the right place to be safe happy and secure."*
> *"I will make the right choice for me."*

Three weeks to the day later, she found a nice condo on a quiet street and within her price range. Her friend Mary had gotten her real estate license on a Wednesday and showed her the place on Thursday. Another friend is her mortgage broker and helped her get a loan at a good rate. She's saving money, and her friends will get a commission on her good fortune.

House Sale

My good friend Dorna wrote:

"Several years ago it was imperative that I sell my home. I put it on the market and waited. Time passed, but no one made an offer to buy, and I grew increasingly discouraged. Then my friend, Ruth, suggested that I create an affirmation to bring about the sale of my home. She said I needed to write this affirmation ten times each day for 21 days, and by the end of this period, my home would be sold.

"Although I held no belief in the power of this kind of validation, I decided to try it anyway, and began to write: 'Today God is directing the perfect person to me to buy my home.' I continued with my affirmation in spite of disbelief, and wrote daily as I had been told to do.

"Time went by with no results, and I found myself saying, 'See, it's all foolishness. My house hasn't been sold. I knew this wouldn't work!' But I kept writing! On day nineteen of affirmation, I received offers from two buyers, and in a matter of weeks, my home was under contract. Today, I am a believer in the power of affirmation, and urge others with skepticism to witness the miracle and become believers, too!"

Even if You're a Skeptic!

You can try affirmations even if you're not convinced. The results may surprise you!

Here's a wonderful testimony from Joe, a man in his sixties, who had never even heard of affirmations until his partner suggested he try them. Joe sent me an e-mail

about the wonderful results of his undertaking and gave it
the wonderful title:

Confessions of a Skeptic

"When my partner D first suggested that we add affirmations to our mix of daily rituals, I was outwardly agree-
able but inwardly skeptical. I thought we already had
enough rituals, beginning with our morning readings to
one another over morning coffee. I had come to treasure
the morning readings, which are equal parts psychology,
philosophy and spirituality. We always discuss the main
point of the reading, in easy and conversational terms,
and it's a great way to prepare for the day.

"But affirmations? What was the point? Rote learning?
Yoga-like concentration on a concept or goal through
repetition of language? Maybe all of that. Let's give it a
try. I concocted my first affirmation: 'I will lose 5 pounds
this month.'

"D patiently explained that affirmations usually aspire
to something grander than small weight losses. Together,
we focused on our current goal of greater harmony in our
daily lives and came up with:

'God, the Spirit of the Universe, is guiding D and me to harmony today.'

"We each committed to write this affirmation twenty
times a day for 21 days. What an experience this effort
became! Every day brought a new emotional ride. Some
days I felt like the mere writing was improving my relations with D. Other days I focused on one word or phrase:
What did I mean by Spirit of the Universe? What is harmony between two separate but respectful partners?

"Other days, I just wrote to fulfill an obligation. I wrote by hand, I used the computer, I wrote on airplanes, in bed, at the desk. When I worked past midnight, I wrote all twenty repetitions before going to sleep, because I feared I might be too tired that evening to do the job. But I always wrote them, I didn't cheat once, and I kept the copies.

"This experience motivated me to try another one right away. I wrote this one on my own: 'I will listen for D's song.' A lot shorter, for one thing. More personally directed, for another. It set a goal that I knew was right for me: to listen more acutely daily for the beauty in my partner's inner life. I found it a pleasure, with few exceptions, to write this affirmation.

"What were the results? In my relations with D, I sense more harmony than we had before, and I hear more music in the air."

Negative Thinking

Mindy, a woman with fourteen years sobriety, wrote that she had been having a terrible time with negative thinking when she was eleven years sober. Her sponsor taught her about affirmations, and they eventually changed her life. He told her to stand in front of the mirror, look into her eyes and tell herself, "I am a powerful woman. I am loving, kind, caring and giving; I can do anything I want to do; I am beautiful just the way I am."

"Did I believe them?" she wrote. "No, of course not. Then about one month later something started to happen. I started to believe what I was telling myself. They were working. This changed my whole life, respective self-esteem, self-respect and self-love. Unbelievable! It worked. Miracles began to happen, one day at a time."

Self-Confidence

A strong, capable woman, Sharon has worked her way up from the lowest ranks in a large, international company. Her latest promotion was to a consulting job in the company where she had been working for many years. While she really wanted the job, she realized that it would cause considerable changes in her life.

A recovering alcoholic, Sharon would be leaving a group of people she had been working closely with for many years who knew she was in recovery and had been very supportive of her personally. She was also leaving a position in which she had been very successful. The new job entailed a great deal of traveling, which meant that she would be away from her five-year-old son for days at a time. The job even included "wining and dining" her new clients, not the best activity for a recovering alcoholic.

The first five months were a big struggle for her. As she began developing new skills, she made many mistakes and was discouraged when her new business associates questioned her suggestions. Hoping for positive support, she attended one of our women's spiritual retreats, at which I emphasized affirmations and meditation. After reading the original version of the *Change Almost Anything in 21 Days,* Sharon created the affirmation:

"I feel strong and confident in my job today."

At first, she struggled to write it every day, but soon it became part of her daily recovery routine. It helped her self-esteem, removed her fear of failure and even helped to remove the perfectionism that she had been burdened with for many years.

When it came time for her performance evaluation, Sharon was thrilled when her boss showed her letters from four of the business people with whom she had consulted. The letters glowed with positive comments relating how she had helped them build their business and achieve great results. She now keeps a very positive outlook and her attitude in this tough business environment is very refreshing.

Mary Jane Beech, founder and director of Bridges Associates, Inc. in Hyannis, Massachusetts, a program for children with special needs and learning disabilities, told me a wonderful tribute for affirmations. Ten years ago, a group of parents identified self-confidence as the most important factor influencing child success and began the "Plant the Seed of Confidence" campaign. They found that affirmations are the best ways to build self-confidence. Many children, parents and teachers report that they feel better using daily affirmations.

A Time for Every Season

Sometimes no matter how much we would like to change something, the timing isn't always in our control. One woman told me the story of how she desperately wanted to be in a relationship. I suggested she write the affirmation: "God is guiding me into a healthy and loving relationship."

She went to a party a week later and met someone she really liked, but didn't hear from that person for some time. Then, one year later, she received an invitation to dinner. The person she met the year before had just not been ready yet, but kept her number, knowing that they

would get together some day. They have been in a
healthy and loving relationship ever since.

There are times when we set the energy into motion by
our affirmation and think that it isn't working, when months
later the job, house or relationship might come through.
And there are times when what we think is right for us just
isn't meant to be. You will always get what you need at the
right time. There's an old saying that God is never late.

Financial Insecurity

Judy worked at a nonprofit agency and could barely
make ends meet on her $18,000 salary. She knew she
was a very good therapist and had wanted to start her
own private practice for years. Fear of financial insecurity
held her back.

I suggested she try an affirmation. She was willing and
wrote, "I am working for myself and earning $18,000 a
year." I proposed she double that figure, and she laughed
and said that was an impossible figure. Within one year
Judy was earning $38,000 and a few years later was
earning over $50,000 and climbing.

Transforming Stress into Gratitude

Mersh has some favorite affirmations that she uses in
times of stress. When she is having a particularly stressful
moment, she stops what she's doing, especially if self-
defeating reactions threaten to erupt. Then she silently
reminds herself of one or more of her favorite affirmations or intentions, such as:

> "I welcome the transformation and relief
> that a simple, intentional moment can
> bring."

"I feel nothing but gratitude for the way in which using this positive power can turn the itchy discomfort of defeat and self-doubt into a welcoming wrap of love, care and possibility."

A few of her others include:

"I am responsible, organized, motivated and productive today."
"With every cleansing breath from the universe, I heal my body as I meditate today."
"I am kind and gentle with myself and others today."
"I make things easy on myself today."

Breaking a Bad Habit

When Nancy's daughter, Joan, was five years old, she began to pick at her fingers, making them very sore. Although Nancy tried many things, such as scolding, painting her daughter's fingernails so they would look pretty, or putting on salve to help them heal, nothing worked.

Nancy followed a nightly ritual since Joan was a baby. She went into Joan's room after she was asleep to whisper soothing words and affirmations to her. Now she began to add the words "you are peaceful with the details of life" from Louise Hay's book *Heal Your Body*. Within a week or two, Joan stopped picking her fingers!

If It Feels Good, Don't Fix It! You Don't HAVE to Stop in 21 Days!

Nan is a lovely young woman afflicted with multiple sclerosis. We had the good fortune to meet long before she was diagnosed, at the age of twenty-nine. During that time she had gotten married, was looking forward to having children and then *crash!* It felt as if her world fell apart when she heard she had MS. Since then, her illness has become much worse, but she has received a variety of treatments, including chemotherapy, and has recently seen a small improvement.

Nan also used the affirmation:

> *"Healing energy is pouring through my entire body with every breath I take."*

She recently sent an e-mail that said, "I haven't followed the 'traditional' 21-day routine. It has been months actually. I can't say how much it's helped physically, whether it's been the chemotherapy or the affirmation, but I suspect it's a combination. I have definitely seen physical improvements. I feel that emotionally and spiritually the affirmation has been extremely beneficial to me. That's why I've continued for so long. I feel now that I have a feeling of control over a very frustrating, fluctuating disease, as well as a tremendous sense of peace and calm. I repeat it to myself after crawling into bed each night. It has become such a routine that I think I'm often unaware of exactly how frequently I have relied on it for a sense of calm and control.

"Initially, I pictured a yellow light of healing that I would breathe in and over the course of time. It has evolved into a visualization with mini-starfish pouring into my body, not

only bringing calm and happiness to my body, but also act-
ing as a kind of mortar, or Band-Aid, in the areas of my
body that have a deterioration of myelin to help transmit
nerve impulses. The only two colors always present are
yellow and purple, kind of a purple background with a
more compact yellow area and yellow/gold starfish."

Nan has begun her meditation practice again, and
"without question it keeps me from being completely
depressed and full of self-pity. There's been a drastic
improvement since then."

Cash Flow

After a very painful divorce from an alcoholic husband,
Caryn found herself in deep financial difficulty and on the
verge of losing her livelihood. She knew she had lost
herself in her marriage and didn't want to lose anymore.

I walked into her store at a moment when she was desperately trying to put everything back together. After she filled
me in on all that she had been through I suggested she try:

"All the money I need is flowing to me."

"I have practiced writing that affirmation almost daily,"
she wrote in an e-mail. "Not only ten times, but as many
times as there were lines on the paper, and I do believe it
helped to make a difference in my life. My attitude
changed and so did many other things. I refinanced my
home and decided to grow my business back and began
writing a new affirmation:

"The will to be fit and strong is within me."

"With this affirmation, I am caring for myself both physically and mentally. My family and my business function better when I have clarity of thought. While I am not fully out of the water yet, I am pretty sure that I will be okay!"

Purpose and Passion

Kate sent an e-mail that she had been writing the affirmations:

"I am waiting patiently for clarity of my purpose."
"God is guiding me to the perfect job for me today."

"Through these affirmations I am thrilled to have focused in on my passion and goals. As a result, I have decided to go to graduate school and get a master's in social work, a field that has always been enormously interesting to me. In my free time I find myself reading self-help, social work, sociology and psychology books. I can't get enough information! I have a B.S. in sociology and psychology and always loved every minute of school. Thank you for the inspiration to tap into my passion again."

Faith

Darlene struggled with her fear of public speaking for many years. She finally reached the point of acceptance that it would never go away and she decided to avoid any situation that involved any speaking before others in groups.

As she became more mature, she realized this fear was holding her back, both socially and at work. I shared with her my story of my own fear of public speaking and gave her the following affirmation:

"God gives me all the courage I need to speak confidently."

While her self-talk told her, "You just don't understand. I'm different and this will not work," she had the gift of desperation and was willing to try anything. She no longer wanted to be ruled by this overwhelming fear!

Darlene wrote this affirmation daily ten times a day for 21 days. She could feel herself start to surrender and she began to believe it. She started to change the way she was thinking.

Every time she heard her inner voices say, "I can't do it," she exchanged it with, "Whatever God wants I am willing to do, just show me the way."

Since Darlene faced this fear, her world is starting to open up. She knows today that she doesn't need to fear anything as long as she has faith and is willing to open her mind to new possibilities.

New Living Space for a Creative Person

Sharon lived with her daughter and son-in-law to save money. At first, it was very pleasant and comfortable and she enjoyed being with her family.

She had her own room, which gave her privacy, and she took great joy in being with her grandchild.

During the time she was writing her affirmations, Sharon was fortunate to get a job dog-sitting in a beautiful house. It was a great opportunity to have twelve days quiet time, during which she could complete one of her projects and be very much at peace.

During that time, Sharon finished a book she was writing and developed a successful newsletter for healers on Cape Cod. Soon, her space began to feel smaller and smaller and she began to crave a place of her own. I suggested the following affirmation:

> *"All the energies of the universe are guiding me to the perfect place for me to live and create and be peaceful."*

Sharon changed it to conform with her own belief system. It is a perfect example of how you can personalize any affirmation you find in the index to make it right for you:

> *"Source is guiding me to the perfect place to live, to create and to be peaceful."*

When she completed the 21 days of her affirmation, her financial situation had changed for the better. She investigated available senior housing and considered moving. This would give her the privacy she needed. When she told this idea to her daughter and son-in-law, they told her they had a surprise for her. They had plans to add on a garage for workspace for her son-in-law and a room upstairs for her! This way she could have her privacy and still enjoy her family, a perfect combination of peace and freedom to continue her creative work, a place to create and be peaceful.

5

Let's Make a Difference!

When enough of us are aware of something,
all of us become aware of it.

Ken Keyes, Jr.

I wrote *5 Minutes for World Peace . . . Forever: A 90-Day Affirmation Plan,* in 1991, during the Gulf War. My intention was to write a 365-page book with daily reflections on world peace, based on the principles of affirmations. Wanting to get it out right away, Health Communications, Inc., published it as a ninety-day plan.

The premise for this book was that if thousands of people read the same page of this book each day, the energy from their thoughts would spread out into the world and we could have world peace. Since thoughts are energy that we send out into the universe, we have the power to change what is going on in the world. This is certainly not a new thought. People have believed in the power of prayers for thousands of years, and prayers are thoughts.

While my book is no longer in print, the concept is as valid as ever.

Thoughts are energy and are so powerful they can change many of the people around us. Remember, thoughts are energy. And energy makes things happen.

Spend a few moments being still and let yourself feeel how powerful one word can be.

PEACE

Let yourself feeel

the effect of just this one word

PEACE

Now imagine thousands of people reading this one word and the lasting effect it would have on each individual as well as on the people with whom they come in contact.

In his book *The Hundredth Monkey*, Ken Keyes Jr. wrote about scientists who had been observing monkeys in the wild for thirty years. In 1952, on the island of Koshima, they provided monkeys with sweet potatoes, which they had dropped in sand. The monkeys liked the taste of the potatoes but found the sand unpleasant. One day, an eighteen-month-old monkey named Imo washed the potatoes in a nearby stream. She taught the trick to her mother and her playmates, who taught it to their mothers. As the story is told, perhaps ninety-nine monkeys learned to wash their sweet potato between 1952 and 1958. One day the one-hundredth monkey learned to wash the potatoes. Suddenly, almost every monkey on the island began to wash their potatoes before eating them. The added energy of this one-hundredth monkey had somehow created a behavioral breakthrough.

But, more amazing, the scientists observed that the act of washing sweet potatoes had jumped over the sea, because the colonies of monkeys on other islands, as far as 500 miles away, began washing their sweet potatoes.

This phenomena is known as "critical mass." When a limited number of people know something in a new way, it remains the conscious property of only those people. However, there is a point at which if only one more person tunes in to a new awareness, a field of energy is strengthened so that new awareness is picked up by almost everyone.

I can't project the condition of our world by the time you read this book. I only know where it is at the time I am writing it. It is summer 2002. There is merciless, tragic fighting going on in the Mideast. We have not recovered from the tragedy of the terrorist attacks of September 11, 2001, and are told there will be more attacks. The stock market is hitting new lows every day and many people are losing their life savings. It is, needless to say, not a very good time.

Whenever you read this, I invite you to join me and make a difference! Turn to "world peace" in the index. Let your heart select one of the affirmations. Write that affirmation on a few index cards. Carry one with you at all times. You can put another one on your mirror so you will see it and read it to yourself every day. Place one on the visor of your car. Place it anywhere else that feels right to you. Quote your affirmation when you end your e-mail. AND WRITE IT AT LEAST ONE TIME A DAY. I'm not asking that you write it ten times, because I know you have other changes you want to make in your life, and if you commit to too much, you might not do anything. So

I suggest, write it AT LEAST ONE TIME. More is better!
Let's do it. Tell your family and friends about this project. It will take less than one minute in your day and who
knows . . . we might see it work in our lifetime!

6

How to Recharge
Your Life with
More Than 500 Affirmations

Now you have read how to use affirmations, when to use affirmations and why to use affirmations. Are you ready to use affirmations? Are you ready to make a change; add something to your life; let go of something in your life?

When you're ready to make a change, turn to the subject of your intentions and find an affirmation that feels good. If none feel right to you, write one of your own. Remember, you don't have to believe it. It is something you are going toward. You're moving in that direction.

Subjects are often interconnected. For example, if you're seeking to find more love in your life, you might look at resentments, to see what or who is filling your heart with anger or pain. Or look at letting go, to see what you are holding on to that is blocking you from feeling love. There's an old saying that if you have one foot in the past and one foot in the future, you can't be in the present moment.

Affirmations for losing weight can be found under addiction, food and weight. A new job affirmation can be found under career or purpose.

If you have the time, it would be wonderful if you could find a quiet place where you won't be interrupted. Sit quietly and meditate for ten or twenty minutes. Meditation helps you to connect with God, Higher Power, Allah, Jesus, Universal Energy, Divine Guidance or anything you want to call the Power that is greater than ourselves. You can connect with your angels, your spirit guides, or whatever you believe works.

Find an affirmation that feels right for you or rephrase it in any way that makes you most comfortable. The affirmations in the index of this book are simply suggestions. Personalize them in any way you wish. Or write your own!

When you become willing to follow these simple instructions, incredible transformations will begin to occur in your life. Watch for miracles!

Let yourself feeel the power of these affirmations and discover how they can change the way you feel. Discover how they can change your life.
If we believe we are going to change, we are going to change!

aahhh!

Abundance

Expect your every need to be met.
Expect the answer to every problem,
Expect abundance on every level.

Eileen Caddy

I have abundance in all areas of my life.
I am open to all the blessings of the universe.
I deserve to have wonderful things happen to me.
I have everything I need today.
Everything I need is flowing into my life today.
The Universe is providing me with _____
    (add your own intention or desire here).
I allow God to provide me with abundance on all levels.

Acceptance

I accept myself just as I am today.
I am willing to accept life on life's terms.
I accept my limitations.
I am learning to accept limitations in myself and others.
I accept my progress today.
I accept others as they are today.

Addictions/See also Compulsions; Food; Habits; Recovery; Weight

I don't gotta even if I wanna.
I feel the joy of being a nonsmoker.
It feels so good to be drug- and alcohol-free!

I am proud of my healthful eating today.
I am free from the desire to _____
    (add your own word(s) here, i.e., overeat, gamble,
    work, control).
I am a sober person today.
I am free from the control of addictions.
I am drug-free today.
I am asking God to remove _____(name addiction).

Aging

One cannot help being old,
but one can resist being aged.

Lord Samuel

I am managing my aging process with grace and
    acceptance.
I am at the perfect age for me today!
I am grateful to be alive at any age!

Angels

My guardian angel is guiding me to my highest good
    today.
Unseen angels are looking after me today and all is
    well.

I have the unconditional love of my guardian angel and
know that all is well in my life today.
With the help of my angel(s), my life is changing in a
positive way today.
With the help of my angel(s), I face any difficult situation and come through easily and effortlessly.

Anger

Remember, every minute spent in anger
is sixty seconds of happiness wasted.

Author Unknown

I am learning to express my anger in healthy ways.
As I breathe in and out, I watch my anger melt away.
I choose to ignore the anger of others.
I am learning to calm down and practice managing my
    anger.
I am learning to give myself emotional distance from
    tension and conflict.

Attitude/See also Feelings

I have a positive and healthy attitude today.
I'm changing my day by changing my attitude.
My feelings are my friends today.
I allow my feelings to change into positive energy today.

Balance

My life is in balance today.
I am balancing my personal, spiritual and professional
  life today.
God is guiding me as I learn to live a well-balanced life.
I take on only what I can handle.
I am learning to balance the demands on my life today.
I am learning to balance work and play.
I can learn to find balance in my life.
It feeels good to be creating a more balanced life.

Body

I love my body today.
I am taking good care of my body today.
God is helping me to accept my body just the way it is.
It feeels so good to put only healthy things into my
  body.
I treat my body with care and respect, knowing that it
  is the home of my soul.
I am taking care of myself mentally, physically and
  spiritually.

Business/See also Success

All the energies of the universe are guiding the people
to buy my product(s) today.

I am creating a successful business that will help me, my
family and others.

Source is guiding people to it now who will benefit from
my work!

God is guiding me to the next step to make my business
more profitable.

My business is flourishing!

Career/See also Guidance; Job; Purpose

It's kind of fun to do the impossible.

Walt Disney

I am moving forward in my career.

I am growing into my career.

I'm finding the perfect career for me.

I'm finding a fulfilling career that is financially
rewarding.

God is guiding me on my career path.

Changes

I always knew that one day I would take this road
but yesterday I did not know today
would be the day.

Julia Cameron

I am worthy of positive changes in my life.
Today I welcome CHANGE as opportunity.
I am open to positive changes in my life today.
Nothing is stopping me from growing today!
I'm learning more quickly to recognize what I cannot
    change.

I'm letting go of all my struggle to change what I cannot change!

I am taking time to reflect and to enjoy the pleasure of new experiences.

I trust that I will know the right time to make changes in my life.

Choices/See Decisions

Commitments

I am fulfilling all my commitments.
I can be trusted to come through today.
I promise only what I can do today.
I keep all my promises today.

Compassionate

If you cannot be compassionate
to yourself, you cannot be
compassionate to others.

Thich Nhat Hanh

I am a caring and compassionate person.
I give compassion freely today.
I am a loving and compassionate person today.
I am grateful for my compassionate heart.

Compulsions/See also Addictions; Food; Habits; Recovery; Weight

I am free from repeating actions that harm me.

I know that saying "no" to addictions is saying "yes" to myself.

As I close the door to compulsive addictions, many other doors open.

God gives me all the strength I need to say no to my compulsive ways.

I am letting go of my need to do unhealthful things.

Confidence/Self-Confidence; Self-Esteem

Today I am fully alive and open to feeling all that there is, knowing that I can handle all that comes my way.

I am a confident person today.

I am confident in my ability to meet challenges today.

I am a dynamic, confident, charismatic, motivating, fearless _____ (add your own word(s) here, i.e., speaker, leader, teacher, singer, writer, etc.).

I have the confidence to express myself openly and freely today.

I have all that I need to do what is good and right in my life today.

I know that confidence grows with each success.

I feeel strong and confident today.

I am learning to trust my own wisdom and give myself
permission to follow it.

I feeel confident in my ability to _____(add your
own word(s) here, i.e., act, speak, pass this test, etc.).

I am choosing to spend time with people who help me
feel confident.

I am growing in self-confidence.

I know what is right for me and I act on it.

Control

I'm letting go of my need to control everything.

I'm learning to do the footwork while God controls my
direction.

I'm learning to let go and let God.

I see my need to control as a block to me today and I
am letting it go.

Courage

Courage is fear that has said its prayers.

Author Unknown

My courage grows as I try new things.
The Universe supports me as I push beyond my fear.
I have the courage of my convictions.
I have all the courage I need to _____
(add your own word(s) here, i.e., take a plane ride,
    apply for a new job, speak up to my boss).
I have all the courage I need today to face my shortcomings.

Creativity

Today my creativity is flowing easily and effortlessly.
I am open to all the creativity of the universe.
God is showing me what a creative person I am.
I am willing to let go of all the blocks to my creativity.

Decisions

My Higher Power guides me in making healthy and positive decisions today.

I am being guided to make positive choices in my life today.

I am making healthy decisions today.

My decisions are positive and for the good of all concerned.

I choose healthy paths today.

I have choices today.

I trust myself to make a good decision.

Difficult Situations

The experiences of life can become our teachers;
the accidental predicaments
of our lives are, in this sense,
spiritual opportunities.

Tara Bennett-Goleman

I have all the strength, support and guidance I need to
   get through this situation.
I am willing to ask a friend to help me through this
   situation.
I make things easy on myself today.
God is guiding me through this difficult time.

I can learn to ask for help when things are tough.

I can get through anything with the help of my Higher Power.

All the energies of the universe are guiding me through this time.

Doubt/See Faith and Trust

Energy

All the positive energies of the universe are pouring
    through me today.

I choose to spend my energy in a balanced way.

My energy is a force for good in the world.

I use my energy to create positive results.

I am directing my energy in positive and loving ways.

I am open to all the positive and loving energies of the
    universe.

God gives me all the energy I need today to do all that
    needs to be done.

Divine energy is flowing through me with every breath
    I take.

God is guiding me in the best use of my energy.

Excitement

I am excited about _____.
I feeel excitement pouring through me as I think about _____.

I am finding healthy and positive things to feel excited about.

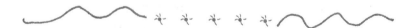

Exercise

My Higher Power gives me all the energy and incentive I need to exercise today.
I feel so good as I take time each day to exercise.
I weigh_____ (insert your intended realistic weight here) and I always have enough time, energy and desire to exercise my body.
I weigh_____(insert your intended, realistic weight here) and I have created my perfect body with slim, trim limbs and firm toned muscle.

faith/See also Problem; Trust

I would rather live my life as if there is a God
And die to find out there isn't,
Than live my life as if there isn't
And die to find out there is.

Author Unknown

My faith is increasing each day.
All the answers I need are coming to me as I need them.
I rely on my faith today.
I turn my will and my life over to the care of God today.
I put my faith in a Power greater than myself.
I have faith that God is guiding me through this time.

Fear

Fear can't stop me from moving forward.
Fear no longer owns me or is a threat to my day.
I'm letting go of my fear today.
I'm turning my fear into faith.
I am moving beyond my fear.
I am free of fear because I have faith.

feelings... all kinds!

Feelings/See also Attitudes

I am not my feelings.
It's okay to feel my feelings.
I do not have to act out on all my feelings.
I'm handling my feelings in a healthy way.

Finances

I am becoming debt-free today.
I am living within my means today.
I am donating more freely to good causes.
All the money I need is flowing to me today.
My business is growing and prospering.
God is guiding me to use my money wisely.
I am financially responsible today.
I am contributing financially to the well-being of others
    whenever possible.
I see money as a way of easing the pain of others.

(Remember to feel the words
as you say them.)

Food/See also Addictions; Compulsions; Habits; Recovery; Weight

God is designing my menu today.
My food choices are healthful today.
I am eating what I need to stay healthy today.
Food is my friend today.
My Higher Power is giving me all the strength I need to
    eat what is good and healthful for me.
I am learning to enjoy eating food that is good for me.

free at last!

Forgiveness/See also Letting Go; Resentments

*I see my ability to forgive as a gift
from God, accepting it as a gift to me.*

Sandy Bierig

I'm moving toward giving forgiveness today.
I'm letting go of all my resentments today.
I accept forgiveness from others.
I am learning how to forgive today.
I am willing to be a forgiving person.
I am devoted to inner peace. I forgive myself no matter
   what.
I let go of my judgments and freely forgive.

Freedom

I am letting go of all my negativity and am becoming free to let joy into my life.

I am letting go of all the blocks that keep me stuck so I can be free to move forward.

I choose to be free today.

No matter what happens to me or around me, I am free inside.

Today I trust that by searching deep within for my own truth, I am discovering the door to freedom and peace.

I am free to be me!

Friends/See also Relationships

I believe that friends are quiet angels who lift us to our feet when our wings have trouble remembering how to fly.

Author Unknown

I take time for my friends today.

I am a good friend.

I am the kind of friend I'd like to have.

I am a loving and considerate friend today.

Fun

I'm taking time to have fun today.
I give myself permission to play, explore and create.
I take some time each day to laugh and play.
I spend at least a few minutes every day with loved ones
    just having fun.
I have harmless fun today.

Generosity

We make a living by what we get,
but we make a life by what we give.

Norman MacEswan

I am growing in my ability to be generous.
I am able to share with others more freely.
I am a generous person!
I feel wonderful when I am able to give freely to others.
I am donating more freely to good causes.

I am more generous with my_____
    (add your own words here, i.e., time, money, self).

I'm generous with my praise and compliments.
I am willing to let go of any fear I have that keeps me
   from being generous.

Goals/See also Plans

The tragedy of life does not lie in not reaching your goal.
The tragedy lies in having no goal to reach.

Benjamin Mays

I am setting realistic goals for me today.
My goals are positive and move me forward on a
  healthy path.
I am willing to set challenging goals for myself.
I am working a little every day to reach my goals.
My goals are for my highest good and for the highest
  good of all.
God gives me all the strength I need to reach my goals.

Gratitude

Gratitude unlocks the fullness of life.
It turns what we have into enough, and more.
It turns denial into acceptance, chaos to order,
confusion to clarity. It can turn a meal into a feast,
a house into a home, a stranger into a friend.

Melody Beattie

I am maintaining an attitude of gratitude today.
I start each day with my gratitude list.
I am grateful for the smallest things today.
Gratitude keeps me connected to the universe.
I can always find something in my life for which to be
  grateful.

grief ... so
heavy ...

Grief

Taking time to grieve brings relief from my pain.
I'm taking all the time I need to grieve.
Grieving is my path out of darkness.
Allowing myself to feel my grief is healing.
God guides me through my grief.
God gives me all the strength I need to handle my grief.

READER/CUSTOMER CARE SURVEY

We care about your opinions! Please take a moment to fill out our online Reader Survey at **http://survey.hcibooks.com**.

As a **"THANK YOU"** you will receive a **VALUABLE INSTANT COUPON** towards future book purchases as well as a **SPECIAL GIFT** available only online! Or, you may mail this card back to us and we will send you a copy of our exciting catalog with your valuable coupon inside.

(PLEASE PRINT IN ALL CAPS)

First Name _____ MI. _____ Last Name _____

Address _____

State _____ Zip _____ Email _____ City _____

1. Gender
- ☐ Female ☐ Male

2. Age
- ☐ 8 or younger
- ☐ 9-12 ☐ 13-16
- ☐ 17-20 ☐ 21-30
- ☐ 31+

3. Did you receive this book as a gift?
- ☐ Yes ☐ No

4. Annual Household Income
- ☐ under $25,000
- ☐ $25,000 - $34,999
- ☐ $35,000 - $49,999
- ☐ $50,000 - $74,999
- ☐ over $75,000

5. What are the ages of the children living in your house?
- ☐ 0 - 14 ☐ 15+

6. Marital Status
- ☐ Single
- ☐ Married
- ☐ Divorced
- ☐ Widowed

7. How did you find out about the book?
(please choose one)
- ☐ Recommendation
- ☐ Store Display
- ☐ Online
- ☐ Catalog/Mailing
- ☐ Interview/Review

8. Where do you usually buy books?
(please choose one)
- ☐ Bookstore
- ☐ Online
- ☐ Book Club/Mail Order
- ☐ Price Club (Sam's Club, Costco's, etc.)
- ☐ Retail Store (Target, Wal-Mart, etc.)

9. What subject do you enjoy reading about the most?
(please choose one)
- ☐ Parenting/Family
- ☐ Relationships
- ☐ Recovery/Addictions
- ☐ Health/Nutrition
- ☐ Christianity
- ☐ Spirituality/Inspiration
- ☐ Business Self-help
- ☐ Women's Issues
- ☐ Sports

10. What attracts you most to a book?
(please choose one)
- ☐ Title
- ☐ Cover Design
- ☐ Author
- ☐ Content

TAPE IN MIDDLE; DO NOT STAPLE

FOLD HERE

Comments

Guidance/See also Career; Job; Purpose

All the energies of the universe are guiding me today.
God is guiding me on my path and my pace today.
I am being guided in positive directions today.
I pray for guidance in all that I do.
I am open to God's plan for me today.
The Universe is providing me with _____
   (add in your own intention or desire here).
I allow God to provide me with abundance on all levels.

Habits/See also Addictions; Compulsions; Recovery; Weight

We are what we repeatedly do.
Excellence, then, is not an act, but a habit.

Aristotle

I am developing healthy habits today.
I am letting go of all the unhealthy habits that kept me
    stuck.

Harmony

He who lives in harmony with himself
lives in harmony with the universe.

Marcus Aurelius

I feel connected to the peace and harmony of the universe.
My home is in harmony today.

I love the harmony in my relationships today.
My life is flowing harmony today.
My Higher Power is showing me how to remove all my
blocks to peace and harmony.

(Remember to feel the words
as you say them.)

Healing/Health

Healing energy is flowing through all the cells of my
body.

I feel vibrant and in good health.
Today I am connecting with my own natural rhythm
   and honoring it.
I am letting go of everything that threatens my health.
I am an instrument of God's healing love.
Healing energy is flowing through me with every breath
   I take.
I'm taking good care of my health today.
I have the power to heal my body.

Honesty/See also Integrity; Principles; Values

*If you want to hear the truth, listen to the heart,
because it doesn't know how to lie.*

Gingerale

I am living an honest life today.
I am one with myself through honesty.
Honesty is my way to freedom today.
I dare to tell the truth no matter what happens.
It feels so good to be truthful in all my affairs.
God guides me to speak the truth.

Independence

I am giving up my need to lean on others.
I am finding my own path today.
I trust myself to the care of myself today.
I am learning to be an interdependent person.
It's sometimes okay to need the help of others.

Inspiration

God gives me all the inspiration I need to have a
   wonderful day.
I feel inspired as I grow on my spiritual path.
I feel inspired to be the very best of who I am.
I feel inspired to _____
   (add your own words here, i.e., write, act, paint, win
   the Olympics).
I'm generous with my praise and compliments.

Integrity/See also Honesty; Principles; Values

If you have integrity, nothing else matters.
If you don't have integrity, nothing else matters.

Alan Simpson,
former U.S. Senator

I live with integrity today.
God guides me on a life filled with integrity.
I follow the voice of my inner spirit.

Intelligence

I have all the intelligence I need today to _____
(add your own word(s) here, i.e., pass this test, do this
   job, write this book).
I am an intelligent person.

Intimacy

I am opening myself to others.
I dare to be intimate today.
I am open to allowing others in today.
I'm letting myself be seen as I am.
I'm willing to let others get close to me.

Intuition

I am learning to trust myself.
There is a special place within me where I find wisdom.
I trust the small voice inside of me.
I dare to follow my intuition.
Today I sit quietly and patiently, waiting to hear my
    intuitive voice, trusting the stirring and encourage-
    ment of my own inner wisdom.

(Remember to feel the words
as you say them.)

Job/See also Career; Guidance; Purpose

*But where is this going to lead me
to make me a more realized person?*

Nicole Kidman

God is guiding me to the perfect job for me today.
I am perfect for this job.
I am in the process of getting the perfect job for me
    today.
I feel strong and confident in my job today!
I am working in a job that benefits people.
My work contributes to the good of humanity.
I am growing in my ability to do my job well.

of boy!

Joy

I feel the joy of _____today. (Insert what is
   appropriate for you, i.e., teaching, running,
   parenting, skateboarding, writing, learning, etc.).
I am open to having joy in my life.
I live joyfully.
I deserve joy today. I feel the joy of living today.
I am finding time to have joy in my life.
I am discovering what brings me joy.
I am willing to let go of anything that keeps me from
   feeling joy in my life.

Judgments

I'm letting go of being judgmental today.
I am learning to live without judging others.
I am accepting others as they are.
As I practice letting go of my judgments, all parts of me
    come together and I feel complete.

Letting Go/See also Forgiveness; Resentments

*But more frequently the task
is one of letting go,
of finding a gracious heart that
honors the changes in life.*

Jack Kornfield

I'm leaving my work at work.
Today I am willing to let go of all anger and resentments
that keep me stuck in tension and in pain.
My past no longer owns me.
I'm no longer a victim of my past.
I am letting go of _____
(insert your own intention here).
Today I am willing to let go and let God work in my life.
I am letting go of all the negative thoughts that limit my
choices.
I'm letting go of my self-imposed burdens today.
I'm letting go of should and ought to today.
I'm letting go of my need to be perfect.
I'm letting go of my need to control everything.
I am at peace with the past.
God is guiding me to let go of all that is blocking me
from feeling peace.

Life

Just to be is a blessing.
Just to live is holy.

Rabbi Abraham Heschel

I am open to new experiences today.
I am willing to live life on life's terms.
I love life today!
I choose to live my life in a positive way.
I am feeling passion in my life today!
I value life as a gift from God.

Love

The experience of love is a choice we make,
a mental decision to see love
as the only real purpose and value in any situation.

Marianne Williamson

Today I choose to see everyone through the eyes of love.

I am growing in love and compassion.

My heart is filled with love and compassion.

I can accept love today.

I choose to give love freely.

I am coming from a place of goodness and love today.

God is removing everything that blocks me from my ability to love and be loved.

I am learning to love without judgment today.

Meditation

The secret of meditation is to become conscious
of each moment of your existence.

Thich Nhat Hanh

I am eager to meditate today.

I have all the time I need to meditate every day.

I am a daily meditator.

Meditation is a gift I lovingly give myself each day.

I release all my resistance and barriers to meditation today.

Meditation brings me closer to my creative source.

My meditation is flowing easily and effortlessly.

I feel myself filled with loving energy as I meditate today.

I seek the knowledge of God's will for me in meditation.

Miracles

*Miracles are instantaneous, they cannot be
summoned, but come of themselves,
usually at unlikely moments and to those
who least expect them.*

Katherine Anne Porter

I am open to all the miracles of this day.
I expect miracles.
I'm hanging in 'til the miracle happens.
I believe in miracles.

Today I have all the courage I need to let go of everything
that is holding me back so that I can step forward and
experience each miracle that is waiting for me.
I am clearing out old confusion and doubt so that I can
see the miracles today.

Money/See Finances

Needs

The Universe is providing me with all my needs today.
All my needs are being met today.
I have everything I need today.

Order

There is Divine Order in my life today.
I am moving toward order and clarity.
I am clearing out the clutter of my life.
My life is full of peace and orderliness.

Parenting

My child is/children are a great source of joy in my life.
I am willing to give my child/children the space
he/she/they need when the time is right.
I am a calm, loving _____
(insert your own word here, i.e., parent, mother,
father, guardian), filled with strength and flexibility,
supporting my children in becoming all that they can
be.

feels so good!

Peace/See also World Peace

*We look forward to the time when the power of
love will replace the love of power.
Then the world will know the blessings of peace.*

William Ewart Gladstone

I am taking the time today to do whatever I need to do
   to bring peace into my life.
I am feeling peace in this very moment.
I feel peace pouring through my entire body.
Peace and relaxation flow through me with every
   breath I take.
Peace is as close as my next breath.
I feel peace at all times.
I am positive and peaceful today.
I am filled with peace and harmony.
I release the illusion of being rushed.
I feel peaceful and serene, knowing that I'll know when
   I need to know.

Perfectionism

*For only in the reality of our imperfection
can we find the peace and serenity we crave.*

Ernest Kurst and Katherine Ketchum

I'm letting go of my need to be perfect.
It feels so good to let go of perfectionism as my goal.
I am looking for progress, not perfection in my life.

Plans/See also Goals

*Affirm: Today I set my intention to remember God.
I awaken asking, "God, what would You have me do
today?" Then I listen for an impulse, idea or directive.
Throughout the day, I welcome God's interruptions,
knowing Spirit has a plan bigger than my own agenda.*

Mary Manin Morrissey

I am planning my day to have time to connect with God
and also with myself.

My plans for today are realistic and manageable.
I look forward to God's guidance when I make my
plans.

$\mathcal{P}$ositive

Since my house burned down
I now have a better view of the rising sun.

Mather Fox

I am positive and peaceful today.
I choose to have positive people in my life today.
I look for the positive in each situation.

(Remember to feel the words
as you say them.)

Prayer/See also Spirituality

Rise with the sun to pray.
Pray alone.
Pray often.
Great Spirit will listen, if you only speak.

Native American Code of Ethics

I take time to connect with my Higher Power every day.
I deepen my connection with God each day through
   prayer and meditation.
I pray for the knowledge of God's will for me and the
   power to carry it out.
I talk to God in the morning to start my day.

Principles/See also Honesty; Integrity; Values

Lead your life so you won't be ashamed
to sell the family parrot to the town gossip.

Anonymous

I live a life based on principles today.
I trust my inner sense of what is right for me.
I do my best to do what is right in all my affairs.

Problem/See also Faith; Trust

God is opening the door for the perfect solution to my
    problem.
The Universe gives me all the answers I need today.

$\mathcal{P}$rocrastination/See also Solitude; $\mathcal{T}$ime

Even if you're on the right track,
you'll get run over if you just sit there.

Will Rogers

I do what needs to be done when it needs to be done.
I do things immediately today.
I do things today so I will have more time tomorrow.

i'm good

Purpose/See also Career; Guidance, Job

Let the beauty you love be what you do.
There are a thousand ways to kneel
and kiss the earth.

Rumi

To find our calling is to find the
intersection between our own deep
gladness and the world's deep hunger.

Frederick Buechner

I am positive and directed and have purpose in my life.
My next step is becoming clear.
I am waiting patiently for clarity of my purpose.
I am finding meaning and purpose in my life.

Recovery/See also Addictions; Compulsions; Food; Habits; Weight

It feeels so good to know I am on my spiritual path to
recovery.
God is guiding me on my spiritual path to recovery.
I am growing every day as I practice the 12 steps of
recovery.

Relationships/See also Friends

*This is the most profound spiritual truth I know:
that even when we're most sure that love
can't conquer all, it seems to anyway.*

Anne Lamott

Today I am finding the good in all the people to whom
I am connected.

I am willing to live in the present moment and not continue to go over regrets and resentments of the past.

Today I am willing to accept people as they are, not as
I would like them to be.

I am finding the perfect partner for me today.

The Universe is guiding me to the perfect partner for
me.

God is guiding me into a healthy relationship.

I am meeting a healthy, positive and available person.

I am attracting positive people in my life today.

I am attracted to positive and loving people, and positive and loving people are attracted to me.

I am a loving _____(insert your own
word here, i.e., partner, friend, parent, daughter,
son, lover, grandmother).

I am a positive and loving person.

I value the role of others in my life today.

I am happy for the success of others.

I am happy to be one among many today.

I surround myself with positive and healthy people
today.

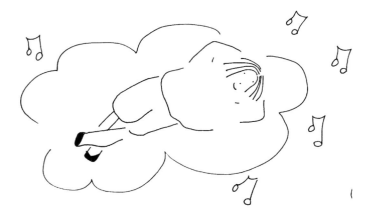

Relaxation/See also School-Related; Teaching

I am leaving my work at work.
I am taking time for me today!
I feel relaxed and calm today.
I am learning to relax today.
I deserve to take time for me today.

Resentments/See also Forgiveness; Letting Go

Avoid hurting the hearts of others.
The poison of your pain will return back to you.

Native American Code of Ethics

I am willing to let go of all the resentments today that
are keeping me stuck in the past.

I am turning over all my resentments to my Higher
Power.

I welcome forgiveness as a way to release me from my
resentments.

Respect

*If I take five minutes out of each day to remember
to treat others the way I want to be treated,
we could accomplish wonderful things together.*

Bob Fishel

I am respected in my profession, and what the Universe
offers me today reflects that.

I deserve to be treated with respect.

I respect and care for my body today.

I treat others with respect.

I respect the differences in people.

(Remember to feel the words.)

Responsibility

I take full responsibility for my life today.

I am responsible for the results of my words and actions.

Today I am responsible for myself and I let others be responsible for themselves.

I am responsible, organized, motivated and productive today.

Safety

I am safe today.
I find safety with my friends and family.
God is keeping me safe.
I deserve to feel safe.
I spend time with people who help me feel safe.
There is always a place where I can go and find safety.
God is guiding me safely on my journey.

graduation day

School-Related/See also
Relaxation; Teaching

I am passing my exams with ease.
I am passing my course with ease.
I am filled with all the knowledge I need to pass this
   test.
I am passing my exam with flying colors.
My mind is relaxed and open to all that I need to learn
   today.
I am focused on my studies.
I get all my homework in on time.
I am a terrific student!
I am finding learning to be fun and exciting.
I am doing the very best I can.
I'm becoming smarter and smarter every day.
I am learning to refrain from judging myself if I have
   trouble with _____
   (insert your own word here, i.e., reading, spelling,
   speaking, writing, typing, computers, etc.).
I am learning to refrain from demeaning myself if some-
   thing is too hard. I can ask for help without feeling
   less than others.

Self-Confidence/See also Confidence; Self-Esteem

I am growing in self-confidence.
I can!
I know, love and trust myself today.
I am equal to the tasks I face.

Self-Esteem/See also Confidence; Self-Confidence

The "self-image" is the key to human personality.
Change the self-image and you change
the personality and the behavior.

Maxwell Maltz, M.D.

I am terrific just the way I am!
I believe in myself today.
I deserve to be treated with love and respect.
I am good enough just the way I am.
Today I dare to be with me and all that I am.
Today I treat myself as my own best friend with gentleness and love.
I value myself today.
My ego is fed in healthy ways.
I celebrate my strengths, abilities and talents.

Self-Pity

I am giving up my need for self-pity today.
I am finding healthy ways to feel good about myself.
God is replacing my self-pity with gratitude.

Shame

I am letting go of the burden of shame in my life.
My past no longer owns me.
I am willing to forgive myself for things I have done in the past.

Shoulds

I'm letting go of my "shoulds" today.
I no longer do things just because someone says I should.
I make choices based on wants, not "shoulds."
My "shoulds" no longer own me.

Simplicity

I'm keeping my life simple today.
God is guiding me in a simple life today.
I'm learning to simply be.

Solitude/See also Procrastination; Time

I welcome the peace, serenity, wisdom and spirituality I find when I take time for solitude.

Everyone can do without me while I take some time for solitude.

It is important that I take time alone to connect with God each day.

I deserve some special time in solitude.

Spirituality/See also Prayer

Affirmations such as
"I am a child of the universe,"
and "God takes care of injustice," or
"I am safe and I trust God's justice,"
turn us in the right direction.

Barbara Berger

I am growing toward others and God today.
God is guiding me on my spiritual path to recovery.
My spirituality is deepening as I take time to pray and
   meditate each day.
I am growing as a spiritual human being.
I am one with God.
I am willing to release everything that is blocking my
   spiritual growth.

Strength

God is giving me all the strength I need today.

Struggle

I am giving up my need to struggle.
I am willing to move forward, in spite of my struggles.

Success/See also Business

I have missed more than 9,000 shots in my career.
I have lost almost 300 games.
On 26 occasions I have been entrusted to take the
game-winning shot . . . and I have missed.
I have failed over and over again in my life.
And that's precisely why I succeed.

Michael Jordan

I am staying with _____
    (insert your own word(s) here, i.e., school, this proj-
    ect, my job, finding a new job) until I succeed.
I am getting more and more successful in_____
    (insert your own word(s) here, i.e., school, work, this
    relationship, my job).
I am a success!
I am successful in all that I do today.
God is guiding me forward to succeed.
I am working toward successful results.
My relationships are successful today.

Suffering

I've outgrown the need to suffer.

12-Step Expression

Surrender

I surrender the things that hold me back.
I can't. God can. I think I'll let God.
I give up my need to do everything alone.

Talents

Use what talents you possess;
the woods would be very silent
if no birds sang except those that sang best.

Henry Van Dyke

I am so grateful for my God-given talents.
I'm developing my God-given talents.
My talents and abilities are valued and needed, and
what the Universe offers me today reflects that.

Teaching/See also Relaxation; School-Related

I am a confident, encouraging and motivating teacher.

I feel the joy of teaching today.

I am grateful for the gift of being able to contribute to the lives of my students.

I feel the joy and enthusiasm that brought me to this profession.

Even though it is not always obvious, my teaching is changing the lives of many of my students.

If there is one student I can help, my day is worthwhile.

on time.
my time.

Time/See also Procrastination; Solitude

I'm doing everything on time today.
I have all the time I need to do everything that is good
   and right in my life today.
I'm taking time for me today.
I have all the time I need to do God's will today.
I am making time today to _____.

Today

I'm living my life one day at a time.
My past no longer owns me.
I have put aside my regrets from the past and fear of the future.
I can do anything for one day.
This is the first day of the rest of my life.

Traffic

I am flexible; I am calm; I am forgiving; I have plenty of time!
I am relaxed and patient.
I leave for appointments in plenty of time to reach them without rushing.
I am arriving at the perfect time.
I am enjoying this extra time to relax.

Travel

God is guiding me safely home.
I ask to be held in God's care when leaving for a trip.
I am traveling safely.
God is in charge of my trip.

Trust/See also Faith; Problem

I'm learning to trust my instincts today.
I'm trusting _____(insert your own
    word(s) here, i.e., God, myself, others, people I love,
    people who care about me).

I'm trusting that my intentions are coming from good and love.

I trust that my Higher Power is guiding me to my next step.

I trust myself today.

I am letting go of doubt, fear, anger and distrust and quietly accept the unknown.

I trust that the Universe is providing for all my needs.

I trust everything is happening for my highest good.

I am being led on the right path for me today, trusting all the details to God.

Values/See also Honesty; Integrity; Principles

I take time to recognize my core values.

I am living my life, consistent with my values.

Weight/See also Addictions; Compulsions; Food; Habits; Recovery

I am in the process of arriving at a healthy weight for me.

I am proud to be eating correctly today.

My Higher Power is guiding me to eat healthy and lose weight.

I weigh _____(put in your own intended, realistic weight) and I maintain my weight easily, eating foods that are healthy and consistent with a slim, trim figure.

I am becoming willing to achieve the perfect weight for me.

I am achieving the perfect weight for me.

I am becoming willing to become willing to get ready to lose weight.

Willingness

I am willing to do everything I can to nurture my body, mind and soul.

I am willing to be a positive and loving person.

God gives me all the willingness I need to grow as a spiritual human being.

I am willing to do everything that is good and right today.

Step One:
I am willing to be willing to _____
(put your own intention here, i.e., give up sweets,
walk one mile daily, study for my exams).
Step two: I am willing to _____
(put your own intention here, i.e., give up sweets, walk
one mile daily, study for my exams).
I can do anything for one day.

World Peace/See also Peace

Let there be peace on Earth and let it begin with me.
I take time each day to pray for world peace.
I know I am making a positive difference in the world today.
Today I am being a little kinder to everyone I meet.
Today I will do my very best to bring peace to my life
    and to the lives of those around me.
I am sending thoughts of peace and love to my world
    family today.
I am connected to all people who are a force of peace
    and light in the universe.
I am bringing peace and serenity to at least one other
    person today.

Worry/See Faith, Fear, Trust and Letting Go

My Personal
21-Day
Journal

Here are 21 pages for your first affirmation. Choose one change you would like to make in your life and begin now!

Remember, they must be:

1. **POSITIVE**
2. Said and felt with **PASSION** and **POWER**
3. Be in the **PRESENT** moment
4. **POSSIBLE**
5. **PERSONAL**

Please don't be too hard on yourself if you miss a day. If you find that you have skipped a day, just start over again with day one.

Whether you are consciously aware of it or not, your affirmations are working for you.

As you write your affirmations, know
that you are in the process of becoming the
author of your own life script!
Congratulations!

Day One

I have all the energy and willingness to write my affirmation ten times today.

_____

_____

_____

_____

_____

_____

_____

_____

_____

_____

_____

_____

_____

_____

_____

_____

_____

_____

Thank you!

Day Two

All the energies of the universe are working for my affirmation today.

_____

_____

_____

_____

_____

_____

_____

_____

_____

_____

_____

_____

_____

_____

_____

_____

_____

_____

_____

_____

Thank you!

Day Three

Everything is flowing easily and effortlessly in my life today.

_____

_____

_____

_____

_____

_____

_____

_____

_____

_____

_____

_____

_____

_____

_____

_____

_____

_____

_____

Thank You!

Day Four

I can feeel positive changes happening in my life today.

_____

_____

_____

_____

_____

_____

_____

_____

_____

_____

_____

_____

_____

_____

_____

_____

_____

_____

_____

_____

Thank you!

Day Five

Positive energy flows through me as I grow on my spiritual path toward love and peace.

_____

_____

_____

_____

_____

_____

_____

_____

_____

_____

_____

_____

_____

_____

_____

_____

_____

Thank You!

Day Six

My Higher Power is working in my life today.

_____

_____

_____

_____

_____

_____

_____

_____

_____

_____

_____

_____

_____

_____

_____

_____

_____

_____

_____

_____

Thank you!

Day Seven

I have new strength and purpose as I continue to write my affirmations.

_____

_____

_____

_____

_____

_____

_____

_____

_____

_____

_____

_____

_____

_____

_____

_____

_____

_____

_____

Thank you!

Day Eight

Positive changes are already happening as I write my affirmations today.

Thank you!

Day Nine

It is powerful to know that I do not make my changes alone.

_____

_____

_____

_____

_____

_____

_____

_____

_____

_____

_____

_____

_____

_____

_____

_____

_____

_____

Thank you!

Day Ten

I am grateful that affirmations work in my life.

_____

_____

_____

_____

_____

_____

_____

_____

_____

_____

_____

_____

_____

_____

_____

_____

_____

_____

_____

_____

_____

_____

Thank you!

Day Eleven

I feeel my affirmation happening with every part of my body and my mind and my spirit.

_____

_____

_____

_____

_____

_____

_____

_____

_____

_____

_____

_____

_____

_____

_____

_____

_____

_____

Thank you!

Day Twelve

As I go through this day, I know that my Higher Power is guiding me.

_____

_____

_____

_____

_____

_____

_____

_____

_____

_____

_____

_____

_____

_____

_____

_____

_____

_____

_____

Thank you!

Day Thirteen

It is exciting to know that my life is moving in a positive and healing direction.

_____

_____

_____

_____

_____

_____

_____

_____

_____

_____

_____

_____

_____

_____

_____

_____

_____

Thank you!

Day Fourteen

I am in the process of releasing all my resistance and doubts and fears so that my affirmation can work in my life today.

_____

_____

_____

_____

_____

_____

_____

_____

_____

_____

_____

_____

_____

_____

_____

_____

_____

_____

_____

Thank you!

Day Fifteen

Everything is happening for goodness and love.

_____

_____

_____

_____

_____

_____

_____

_____

_____

_____

_____

_____

_____

_____

_____

_____

_____

_____

_____

Thank you!

Day Sixteen

I am doing the footwork today.

_____

_____

_____

_____

_____

_____

_____

_____

_____

_____

_____

_____

_____

_____

_____

_____

_____

_____

_____

_____

Thank you!

Day Seventeen

My Higher Power is guiding me on my path and my pace today.

_____

_____

_____

_____

_____

_____

_____

_____

_____

_____

_____

_____

_____

_____

_____

_____

_____

_____

_____

_____

Thank you!

Day Eighteen

My purpose for this day is to become more and more clear as I write my affirmations.

_____

_____

_____

_____

_____

_____

_____

_____

_____

_____

_____

_____

_____

_____

_____

_____

_____

_____

_____

_____

Thank you!

Day Nineteen

I have all the energy that I need to do that which is good and right in my life.

_____

_____

_____

_____

_____

_____

_____

_____

_____

_____

_____

_____

_____

_____

_____

_____

_____

Thank you!

Day Twenty

I am the author of my own life script today.

_____

_____

_____

_____

_____

_____

_____

_____

_____

_____

_____

_____

_____

_____

_____

_____

_____

_____

_____

Thank you!

Day Twenty-One

I am writing my affirmation ten times a day for 21 days.

_____

_____

_____

_____

_____

_____

_____

_____

_____

_____

_____

_____

_____

_____

_____

_____

_____

Thank you!

Notes

Affirmations Index

About the Author

Ruth Fishel, M.Ed., is a prolific author, national retreat and workshop leader and meditation teacher. Her books include: *Time for Joy, The Journey Within, Hang In 'Til the Miracle Happens, Stop! Do You Know You're Breathing?* and *Precious Solitude.* Fishel has also developed Spiritlifters, a line of inspirational greeting cards, drawing on the messages in her books. Her books take the reader on a marvelous journey through pain and loss to inspiration and hope. They provide the reader with a gentle path to growth, peace, and love of self, others and God.

Books and Tapes by Ruth Fishel

Hang in 'Til the Miracle Happens
Precious Solitude
Stop! Do You Know You're Breathing? Simple Techniques
   for Teachers and Parents to Reduce Stress and Violence in
   the Classroom and at Home
The Journey Within: A Spiritual Path to Recovery
Time for Joy, daily meditation and affirmations which has
   sold over 300,000 copies
Time for Thoughtfulness
Take Time for Yourself!
Cape Cod Memories
Memories of the Florida Coast

AUDIOTAPES

Time for Joy
You Can't Meditate Wrong
Transforming Your Past into Presents
*Guided Exercises for Deepening Your Meditation
   Experience*
The Journey Within
Discovering Your Source of Peace

   For more information about Ruth's workshops, retreats, books,
tapes and greeting cards write to *spirithaven@spirithaven.com*, go
to her Web site *www.spirithaven.com* or call her at 508-420-5301